ALL IN THE DANCES

ALSO BY TERRY TEACHOUT

• •

A Terry Teachout Reader

The Skeptic: A Life of H. L. Mencken

City Limits: Memories of a Small-Town Boy

Beyond the Boom:
New Voices on American Life, Culture, and Politics
(editor)

Ghosts on the Roof:
Selected Journalism of Whittaker Chambers, 1931–1959
(editor)

TERRY TEACHOUT

ALL IN THE DANCES

A BRIEF LIFE OF

George Balanchine

HARCOURT, INC.

Orlando   Austin   New York   San Diego   Toronto   London

www.HarcourtBooks.com

Library of Congress Cataloging-in-Publication Data
Teachout, Terry.
All in the dances: a brief life of George Balanchine/
Terry Teachout.—1st ed.
p. cm.
Includes bibliographical references and index.
ISBN 0-15-101088-9
1. Balanchine, George.   2. Choreographers—United States—
Biography.   I. Title.
GV1785.B32T43 2004
792.8'2'092—dc22   2004009226

Frontispiece art: George Balanchine and Igor Stravinsky rehearsing
Diana Adams and Arthur Mitchell in the pas de deux of *Agon*, 1957.
Photo © Martha Swope, used by kind permission of the photographer.
Insert photographs by Fred Fehl by permission of Gabriel Pinski.

Text set in Janson MT
Designed by Linda Lockowitz

Printed in the United States of America

First edition
A C E G I K J H F D B

To my friends in the second seat

Alane, Alicia, Anne, Anya,
Bruce, Chika, Daphne, Deidre,
Dick, Erica, Heather, Julie,
June, Karen, Kate, Kendra,
Laura, Lexi, Lisa, Liz, Lu,
Margo, Maria, Mary, Meg,
Megan, Patch, Peggy, *and* Steph

and in memory of Anita *and* Nancy

We dare to go into the world where there are no names for anything.

GEORGE BALANCHINE

in conversation with Jerome Robbins

· ·

After I retired from dancing, I was sitting on the bench with Balanchine at the School of American Ballet while he rehearsed. As they were working, he said to me, "You know, those men in Tibet up in the mountains. They sit nude in the cave and they drink only water through straw and they think very pure thoughts." I said, "Yes, the Tibetan monks. The lamas." He said, "Yes. You know, that is what I should become. I would be with them." And then he looked around and said, "But unfortunately, I like butterflies."

RUTHANNA BORIS

I Remember Balanchine

Contents

Preface

....

*T*HIS IS A SHORT BOOK about a great man who lived a long life. It is not a full-scale biography and makes no pretense of thoroughness or originality, least of all in its discussions of George Balanchine's ballets, many of which go unmentioned or are discussed only in passing. Nor did I write it for the edification of longtime balletgoers (though I hope it may possibly be of some interest to them). Instead, I had in mind a reader who has just seen his first ballet by Balanchine, or is about to do so, and wants to know something about Balanchine's life and work and how they fit into the larger story of art in the twentieth century. Accordingly, I have used an absolute minimum of technical language, so as to be as intelligible as possible to the interested layperson. I would very much have liked to read a book such as this after I saw my first *Concerto Barocco* in 1987, and so I have also kept in mind myself when younger, as well as the many people whom I have since taken to see *their* first Balanchine ballets.

Because this book is deliberately informal in tone, I have omitted source notes, but I have drawn extensively on the published writings of those who knew Balanchine well, and some of their books are listed in the bibliography, along with others that deepened my understanding of a man I never met (though I have been lucky enough to know a few people who knew him). In addition, I wish to acknowledge Lynn Chu, who first suggested that I write a brief life of Balanchine; André Bernard and David Hough, who saw the results into print with scrupulous care; Meital Waibsnaider, who helped me select the photos; Robert Greskovic, a uniquely generous colleague without whose encouragement I would never have started writing about dance; Betsy Pochoda, who persuaded me to write about it for a mass audience and insisted that I do so in a lively, accessible way; Arlene Croce, from whose criticism I learned much of what I know about Balanchine; Amanda Vaill, author of a forthcoming biography of Jerome Robbins based on his private papers, who discussed her important findings with me at length; and Robert Weiss, with whom I have spent many illuminating hours talking about Balanchine and his work. My heartfelt thanks to one and all—and to Kyra Nichols, who first showed me exactly how beautiful George Balanchine's dances can be.

ALL IN THE DANCES

1 · THE UNKNOWN GIANT

···

*J*N 1987 I WENT TO LINCOLN CENTER TO WATCH
New York City Ballet dance *Concerto Barocco,*
a ballet by George Balanchine set to Bach's Two-Violin
Concerto. I knew the music well, having played one of
the solo parts in high school, but except for an isolated
Nutcracker seen on a college trip to New York, *Barocco*
(as dancers and regular balletgoers call it) was my first
Balanchine ballet. Indeed, I hadn't seen very many ballets of any kind, nor was I much impressed with the
ones I had seen. So far as I could tell, they consisted for
the most part of thin women in white skirts pretending
to be birds, fluttering through elaborately costumed
pantomime shows whose quaint plots were too silly to
take seriously. I didn't know a lot about Balanchine, but
I'd just seen a TV documentary about him that led me

to believe that his dances were different, so I decided to give *Concerto Barocco* a try, in much the same spirit of adventure that might have led another person to go to the Museum of Modern Art, or to a jazz club.

The New York State Theater, New York City Ballet's headquarters since 1964, doesn't exactly inspire aesthetic confidence, at least not at first glance. A vast shoe box of glass and dirty travertine marble designed by Philip Johnson, it is squat on the outside and strange on the inside. The public areas are full of undistinguished modern sculptures. A monstrous spherical chandelier dangles threateningly from the gold-plated ceiling. The proscenium arch is topped with an ornament that looks like the leatherette dashboard of an early sixties mid-price sedan, while the five horseshoe-shaped rings that overlook the orchestra seats are faced with circular lamps that bear a distinct resemblance to the headlights of the same sort of car. The balconies are too high, the auditorium too deep, and unless you're lucky enough to be sitting in the first fifteen rows of the orchestra, you feel as though the stage is a mile or two away. It's not at all the sort of place where one might go expecting a revelation—though that was what lay in store for me.

At five minutes past eight, the houselights went down and the curtain flew up, revealing eight young women dressed in simple white ballet skirts, standing in front of a blue backdrop. The scrappy little band in the pit slouched to attention, the conductor gave the downbeat, and the women started to move, now in time to Bach's driving beat, now cutting against its grain. As the solo violinists made their separate entrances, two more women came running out from the wings and began to dance at center stage. Their steps were crisp, precise, almost jazzy. For a moment I was confused. The stage was bare, and the dancers' unadorned costumes offered no clue as to who they were or what they were doing, though I could tell that they weren't "acting," not in any conventional sense. They made no obviously theatrical gestures, exchanged no significant glances, yet I felt sure they were telling some kind of story. Was I missing the point? All at once I understood: the *music* was the story. The dancers were mirroring its complex events, not in a singsongy, naively imitative way but with sophistication and grace. This was no dumb show, no mere pantomime, but sound made visible, written in the air like fireworks glittering in the night sky. When it was over, eighteen breathless minutes later, the audience broke into friendly but routine applause, seemingly unaware that it had witnessed a miracle. Rooted in my seat, eyes wide with astonishment, I asked myself, *Why hasn't anybody ever told me about this? And what kind of man made it?*

I have heard similar words—sometimes the very same ones—from almost everyone I've taken to see New York City Ballet since then. Rarely do Balanchine's ballets fail to amaze a first-time viewer. The only difference is that while I already had a vague idea of who George Balanchine was in 1987, most of the people who now accompany me to the ballet do not.

Within the tight little world of dance, of course, he is a titan. For all intents and purposes, the history of modern ballet starts with his *Apollo* (1928, music by Stravinsky) and *Prodigal Son* (1929, music by Prokofiev), and New York City Ballet, the company he founded, has performed his work continuously from 1948 on. But what of the larger world of art and culture? New York City Ballet no longer gets written about much in the national press, nor does it appear on television. I know few art-conscious Manhattanites who go to its performances more than sporadically—or to any other dance performances, for that matter. Nowadays there are no "hot tickets" in dance, no events that attract the attention of a truly general audience, and few at which artists from other fields are likely to be seen. For the most part, ballet and modern dance have retreated to the periphery of American cultural consciousness, just as dance criticism has all but vanished from the pages of American magazines; you don't have to know who Balanchine was, or what he did, in order to be deemed culturally literate. Most of my acquaintances regard my love of dance as a harmless idiosyncrasy, and when I assure them that Balanchine was every bit as important as, say, Matisse, they look at me as though I'd tried to tell them that Raymond Chandler was as important as Proust.

During Balanchine's lifetime, though, such comparisons were commonplace (though they were more often made with Picasso, an artist with whom he had far less in common). Back then it didn't seem odd for Arlene Croce to declare in the pages of the *New Yorker* that "if George Balanchine were a novelist or a playwright or a movie director instead of a choreographer, his studies of women would be among the most discussed and most influential artistic achievements of our time." For now that dance is largely ignored by the media, it's easy to forget that there was a time when "everyone" in New York went to New York City Ballet—and not just the beau monde, either, but poets, painters, playwrights, composers, even intellectuals, all of whom went because they knew Balanchine to be a genius at the peak of his powers. In his review of the premiere of *Agon* (1957, music by Stravinsky), the great dance critic Edwin Denby mentioned in passing that "Marcel Duchamp, the painter, said he felt the way he had after the opening of *Le Sacre.*" One need not admire Duchamp to admit the force of his comparison to the epochal premiere of *The Rite of Spring,* the 1913 ballet score by Igor Stravinsky that opened the door to musical modernism, or of the fact that so pivotal a figure in the history of art took the trouble to be present on both occasions. Nor was Balanchine known only to the illuminati. In 1954 he choreographed Tchaikovsky's *Nutcracker* for New York City Ballet and appeared on the cover of *Time.* From then until his death in 1983, and especially after his company took up residence at Lincoln Center, he was one of the best-known artists in America. To be sure, his was far from the biggest name in dance, for those were the days of the "dance boom," the dizzy quarter-century-long interlude when Edward Villella danced on the *Ed Sullivan Show,* Jerome Robbins ruled Broadway, and the defections of Rudolf Nureyev and Mikhail Baryshnikov were front-page news everywhere. Still, a star he most definitely was, not least because of his many collaborations with the legendary composer of *The Rite of Spring.* Balanchine and Stravinsky had worked together as far back as *Apollo,* and in 1972, the year after Stravinsky's death, New York City Ballet put on a weeklong Stravinsky Festival at which twenty new ballets were presented, among them *Duo Concertant, Stravinsky Violin Concerto,* and *Symphony in Three Movements,* three of Balanchine's supreme achievements. And the choreographer was not considered a mere theatrical valet to his older colleague, either. In most of what was written and said about the two men between 1948 and 1983, it was taken for granted that they were peers, and more than enough tastemakers had seen Balanchine's work to make the assumption stick.

Times have changed, and while Stravinsky remains a cultural icon, Balanchine is barely more than a distinguished shadow, the unknown giant of modern art. Yet he is omnipresent, not merely in the New York State Theater but wherever dancers are to be found. If his name is now less familiar to the general public, his work is performed far more widely than it was during his lifetime. Some two dozen of his ballets are danced by companies around the world, many of which are led by men and women who worked closely with him in their youth. *Barocco, Apollo, Prodigal Son, Serenade, Ballet Imperial, Symphony in C, The Four Temperaments, Divertimento No. 15, Agon, Jewels, Stravinsky Violin Concerto:* these are, with *Swan Lake, Sleeping Beauty,* and *Giselle,* the true "classics" of the present-day ballet repertory, the staples whose presence on a program is a guarantee of artistic seriousness and technical accomplishment. As you read these words, it's more than likely that someone somewhere is seeing one of them for the first time, and probably asking the same questions I asked myself in 1987. How, then, can it be that *Barocco, Apollo,* and *Agon* are not as celebrated as, say, *The Rite of Spring* or *Remembrance of Things Past*? And—just as important—what singular manner of man called these astonishing works into being?

ONE REASON WHY Balanchine is not as famous as he should be is that mere words, no matter how precise or evocative, can do little more than suggest the emotional effect produced by looking at one of his ballets. For one thing, the works themselves are kaleidoscopically varied. Some, like *Agon* and *Episodes* (1959, music by Webern), are knotty and spare, seemingly as abstract as a painting by Mondrian, though Balanchine disliked that adjective, preferring to call them "plotless." ("Dancer is not a color," he would say in his sniffy, Russian-scented English. "Dancer is a person.") Others, like *Ballet Imperial* (1941, music by Tchaikovsky) and *Symphony in C* (1947, music by Bizet), are resplendently festive, and a few, including *The Nutcracker* and a full-evening dance version of *A Midsummer Night's Dream* (1962, music by Mendelssohn), have story lines fanciful enough to enrapture a nineteenth-century balletomane. Several of his plotless ballets are spectacular crowd-pleasers cunningly engineered to send an audience home happy. *Stars and Stripes* (1958), set to the marches of John Philip Sousa, ends with a giant American flag fluttering in the breeze. Balanchine was proud of his ability to please the public, which he believed to be an indispensable part of the choreographer's craft. In the thirties and forties, he even worked on Broadway and in Hollywood, staging dances for *On Your Toes, Cabin in the Sky,* and *Where's Charley?* in between ballet assignments. As he said time and again, "You can't be like the cook who can cook only two dishes: you must be able to cook them all."

Balanchine may not have invented the plotless ballet, but he grasped its expressive possibilities more completely than anyone else, before or since, and the key to these dances is invariably to be found in their scores, be they by Sousa or Webern. During his early years as a member of the Maryinsky Theater's corps de ballet, he simultaneously studied music across the street at the St. Petersburg Conservatory, where he majored in piano; took lessons on violin, French horn, and trumpet; and learned how to read orchestral scores and prepare his own piano reductions of instrumental works by Berg and Stravinsky. (He would even become a passable conductor, popping into the New York City Ballet pit from time to time to lead the company orchestra.) When he began to make dances, he used his theoretical knowledge and hands-on experience of music in an unprecedented way. Instead of concocting redundant visual equivalents of the rhythmic surface of a symphony or concerto, he plunged into its inner structure, moving his dancers in silent counterpoint to its unfolding action. He made no bones about placing music at the center of his modernized version of nineteenth-century classical ballet—which came, logically enough, to be known as neoclassicism:

> I can always invent movement, and sometimes it can be fitted into the right place, but that is not choreography. It is the music that dictates the whole shape of the work. I do not believe in the permanence of anything in ballet save the purely classical. Classicism is enduring because it is impersonal. . . . Choreographic movement is an end in itself, and its only purpose is to create the impression of intensity and beauty.

Yet his plotless ballets have something in common beyond their reliance on music: no matter how involved their steps may be, the viewer comes away remembering not the skill of the dancers but the inexplicable occurrences scattered generously throughout each dance. Jerome Robbins, who worked alongside Balanchine at New York City Ballet for nearly four decades, observed with admiration that "Balanchine's ballets are all full of the most extraordinary encounters and events." One such event takes place in the slow movement of *Concerto Barocco*. As the music begins, one of the two ballerinas leaves the stage, replaced by a man who dances a pas de deux with her partner. What happens next has been beautifully described by Edwin Denby:

> Against a background of chorus that suggests the look of trees in the wind before a storm breaks, the ballerina, with limbs powerfully outspread, is lifted by her male partner, lifted repeatedly in narrowing arcs higher and higher. Then at the culminating phrase, from her greatest height he very slowly lowers her. You watch her body slowly descend, her foot and leg pointing stiffly downward, till her toe reaches the floor and she rests her full weight at last on this single sharp point and pauses. It is the effect at that moment of a deliberate and powerful plunge into a wound, and the emotion of it answers strangely to the musical stress.

Such emotive language would scarcely have been justified by a purely academic combination of steps, yet the sequence of events that Denby describes appears to have no literal "meaning." Is it derived from the music? So it seems—yet once again, there is nothing explicitly imitative about what Balanchine makes his dancers do. Perhaps the best way to explain it is to say that they do what music does and words cannot. "The thoughts which are expressed to me by music that I love," Felix Mendelssohn once remarked, "are not too indefinite to be put into words, but on the contrary, too *definite*." So, too, with Balanchine, whose choreographic thoughts are extraordinary precisely because they cannot be translated into mere words.

Not surprisingly, Balanchine was reluctant to ascribe specific meanings to his plotless dances. Direct questions he deflected with evasive wit ("It's about fifteen minutes long"), preferring to let the steps speak for themselves, no doubt for the same reason that Henry James left to the reader's horrified imagination the particular evils done by Peter Quint and Miss Jessel to Miles and Flora in *The Turn of the Screw:* "Make him *think* the evil, make him think it for himself, and you are released from weak specifications." In the same way, Balanchine's ballets allow the viewer to think for himself—to see in their music-driven movement whatever occurrences he cares to see—and gain immeasurably in their richness of implication precisely because of their near-complete lack of "weak specifications."

On occasion, though, he let the mask of discretion slip. In the last movement of *Serenade* (1934, music by Tchaikovsky), a man walks from the wings to center stage, accompanied by a woman who shields his eyes with her hand. They meet a second woman lying on the ground. He dances tenderly with her, then departs with the first woman, eyes covered once again. You feel instinctively that this fleeting encounter, perhaps the most poignant in all of Balanchine, must "mean" something—but what? One evening in 1959, after a performance of *Serenade*, the choreographer struck up a conversation with Bernard Taper, his first biographer, and said without prompting that the scene in question had been inspired by a statue of Eros. "It's like fate," he said. "Each man going through the world with his destiny on his back. He meets a woman—he cares for her—but his destiny has other plans."

Does it add to our understanding of *Serenade* to have so bald an explanation of its "meaning," even from the man who made it? Perhaps not. The last movement of *Serenade* "means" what you think it means at the moment you're watching it. Still, it's hard to see Balanchine's plotless ballets as abstract after hearing what he had to say about *Serenade*. Modern, yes: *Serenade* and *Swan Lake* are recognizably related, but one remains firmly rooted in the nineteenth-century ideal of literal representation while the other floats free of it. Even at his most romantic, Balanchine was ever and always the modernist, consciously innovating in order to refresh and renew the great tradition in which he was raised. "Romanticism you have to get from God," he told his dancers. "My business is to show you form." He was the first ballet choreographer to forge a truly modern movement vocabulary, and among the first to find a visual counterpart to the acerbities and angularities of such composers as Stravinsky, Prokofiev, Hindemith, Schoenberg, Webern, and Ives. Yet he was right to shun the reductive label of abstractionist, for his dances, however aggressively modern looking they may be, are *human* dramas, peopled by recognizable creatures of flesh and blood who live and die—and love. "Put a man and a girl on the stage and there is already a story," he said. "A man and two girls, there's already a plot."

THE MAN WHO created these all-too-human ballets led a life outwardly uneventful, at least by the standards of the best-seller list. He fled the Soviet Union in 1924, settling first in Europe and then in New York City, where he started a dance school and a series of ballet companies. For the rest of his days, he made and rehearsed dances. That was all there was to it, he claimed. Asked on one occasion by a journalist to sum up his life, he replied, "It's all in the programs."

Yet there was far more to Balanchine's life than work. Not only did he make dances, but he fell in love with the women who danced in them. He married four times and lived with a fifth woman, all of them ballerinas, and before, during, and after these relationships, he pursued other dancers, at first successfully, then less so. That, too, was in the programs. Alexandra Danilova had been Balanchine's lover in the years before he made *Serenade*, and to her he later offered an even more personal elaboration of its meaning than the one he gave Bernard Taper. As she recalled in her autobiography:

> I danced the first girl, who enters at the beginning. She is a butterfly, having romances with everybody. And then along comes a married man with his wife: they walk, and in their path is this girl. The man has an attraction for her, they dance, but for him it isn't serious, and in the end he continues along the road with his wife. The girl is seeking, suffering, and then she is alone, turning to her friends. I asked Mr. B., and this was his explanation.* And somehow, I think the part I danced— that girl was me.

His romances were complicated, sometimes hurtful, and on one occasion tragic. Tanaquil Le Clercq, Balanchine's fourth wife, was forced from the stage by illness in 1956, at the height of her career. Thirteen

---

*Balanchine's dancers, even those with whom he socialized after hours, usually referred to him as "Mr. Balanchine" or "Mr. B."

years later he divorced her in the hopes of persuading a younger ballerina, Suzanne Farrell, to marry him. Instead, Farrell married another dancer and left New York City Ballet, after which Balanchine made a dance called *Who Cares?* (1970, music by Gershwin). No one who knew him believed it for a moment. "Woman is the goddess, the poetess, the muse," he had said in 1965. "That is why I have a company of beautiful girl dancers. I believe that the same is true of life, that everything a man does he does for his ideal woman. You live only one life and you believe in something and I believe in a little thing like that." He cared, desperately.

A man capable of blithely tossing off such statements to a reporter could never have been called dull, and Balanchine was by all accounts fascinating, if ultimately impossible to know. He adored everything about America, from the dancing of Fred Astaire and Ginger Rogers to the Western movies that inspired him to wear string ties, plaid shirts, and dapper checkered vests that made him look like a riverboat gambler. In his middle age he resembled James Mason, the English actor who played the suave, ruthless villain in Alfred Hitchcock's *North by Northwest*, and he was capable of a similar ruthlessness in both his private and professional lives (insofar as the two could be told apart). Any number of dancers foolish enough to ask why he had taken away one or more of their prized roles were told, bluntly and unanswerably, that they were "too old." And for all the delight Balanchine took in his adopted country and all the slapdash, heavily accented flair with which he spoke its language, no one ever mistook him for an American. "He read the *Daily News* and ate in coffee shops," Edward Villella noted with wonder, but his democratic demeanor stopped at the stage door. He ruled New York City Ballet like a not-always benevolent despot—though his whims were usually tempered by his cool practicality—and more than one of his fellow Russians compared him to Joseph Stalin, another ruthless Georgian who, like Balanchine, was given to casual cruelty and paranoia. Not that anyone dared say such things to his face: Balanchine was the quintessential Soviet émigré, anti-Communist to the bone and religious to boot, never wavering from the Russian Orthodox faith into which he was born. "Religion is primarily faith," he said in old age, "and people today are used to treating everything skeptically, mockingly. That cannot be. You can't test faith."

Not dull, not simple—and yet when it came to the one thing about Balanchine that mattered most, there was little to tell. He worked briskly and without fuss, temperament, explanations, or apparent preparation, so self-confident that he would even allow visitors to sit on bleachers and watch him make a dance. The preparation had already taken place during the long hours he spent listening to and thinking about the music he chose to choreograph. "He once said to me," Villella recalled, "that he had twenty scores in his head at any given time, and when the time was right, with the finances, the personnel, he would say, 'O.K., now is the time to do this.'" When the time came, he went to work, and no sooner did he enter the studio than steps poured out of him like water from a hose. It took him thirty-nine hours of rehearsal to make *Theme and Variations* (1947, music by Tchaikovsky), one of his most popular ballets—less than two weeks' worth of studio time, from start to finish.

Small wonder that many of those who witnessed such improbable feats of creativity described them in near-mystical terms. In the words of Boris Kochno, who wrote the libretto for *Prodigal Son:*

> He started doing this movement and that, showing the dancers what they had to do. Then at a certain moment it became something much more than just himself and his ideas. He started to work as a somnambulist, without knowing what he was doing. And all this was quickly done, with the greatest assurance. When he finished, he would sit and ask the dancers to show him what he had done, and he

would seem to be very astonished. That is what I call inspiration.

Balanchine himself preferred the no-nonsense language of a craftsman. "I don't create or invent anything, I assemble," he said over and over again. "God already made everything—colors, flowers, language." Like Stravinsky, he saw himself less as an artist than an artisan, a carpenter of movement, and what he prided himself on was not his genius (a word he never used about himself) but his skill and reliability. "Choreography, finally, becomes a profession," he wrote in 1954. "In making ballets, you cannot sit and wait for the Muse. Union time hardly allows it, anyhow. You must be able to be inventive at any time." That was George Balanchine's exalted notion of professionalism: to make masterpieces on union time.

2 · ENCOUNTERS AND EVENTS

....

*B*ALANCHINE SPENT the second half of his life working with young American dancers, most of them sketchily educated, who knew nothing of the first half of his life beyond what he told them himself. To them he was an enigma, an unpretentious, self-contained tyrant who never raised his voice, making his ballets as casually as another man might wind his watch. Though he ate pizza, ironed his own shirts, and took as his third wife an Osage Indian named Tallchief, they saw him as the living embodiment of a lost world of czarist elegance they could barely imagine, and when they sought to describe him to outsiders, they almost always resorted to the word "aristocratic." In fact, Georgi Melitonovich Balanchivadze was the son of a ne'er-do-well musician who struck it rich in a lottery, frittered away his winnings, and was arrested for debt.

Meliton Antonovich Balanchivadze, the son of a Russian Orthodox bishop and a pupil of Nikolai Rimsky-Korsakov, the celebrated composer of *Scheherazade* (and teacher of Igor Stravinsky), collected the folk songs of his native Georgia and wove them into his own compositions, paying the rent by serving as the leader of folk choirs that toured Russia, singing his arrangements of the songs he had collected. He never distinguished himself as a composer—his entry in the second edition of the *New Grove Dictionary of Music and Musicians* is not quite a half column long—but when he won 200,000 rubles in the Russian state lottery in 1901, three years after his second marriage, he made a splash of a different sort. The Balanchivadzes lived in St. Petersburg, at whose legendary conservatory Meliton had studied, and Russia's most cosmopolitan city proved a suitable place for the disposal of large amounts of money. He moved his family into a twelve-room apartment, bought a summer house in Finland, made loans to his poor friends, invested in a restaurant, built a factory, and subsidized the publication of the letters of Mikhail Glinka, Russia's first major classical composer. Like most artists, though, he had no head for business, and within a few years he went broke. Balanchine liked to claim that his father had been thrown into debtors' prison, a tall tale that his first biographer swallowed whole. The truth was less spectacular: Meliton spent four months under house arrest, after which he resumed the precarious middle-class existence of a composer and choirmaster.

Beyond making for a good story, Meliton's folly was memorable mainly for its effect on Georgi, who was born on January 22, 1904, during his parents' brief hour of affluence. Once the lottery money had been squandered, Meliton could no longer afford to send his three children to school. If they were to make their way in the world, they would have to be educated at the state's expense. Georgi was expected to enter the Imperial Naval Academy of St. Petersburg, but the rolls were full on the day the nine-year-old boy applied, so instead he accompanied Tamara, his older sister, to her audition for a place as a ballet student in the Imperial Theater School of St. Petersburg. Then as now, young boys who wanted to become dancers were hard to find, and a faculty member suggested that Georgi try his luck as well. Not for the first or last time, the sibling who auditioned on a lark turned out to be more talented than the one who sought admission. Both children were accepted, but the less gifted Tamara soon dropped out, leaving her brother to fend for himself.*

---

*Andrei, Balanchine's younger brother, would become a respected academic composer, though his music is unknown outside Russia and is now largely forgotten.

As an adult, Balanchine had little to say about his parents, but we know that Maria Balanchivadze, his mother, was his first piano teacher—he began playing at the age of five—and that he spent little time with his father, who was usually traveling with one of the choirs he led. We also know that Georgi's affectionate memories of the "fantastic" St. Petersburg Christmases of his childhood made their way into the family party portrayed in the first act of his version of *The Nutcracker,* and that the highly theatrical Russian Orthodox church services he attended around the same time made an equally lasting impression on him. Above all he remembered the city of his birth. "He who did not live in the years before the revolution," Talleyrand said of France's ancien régime, "cannot understand the sweetness of living." Balanchine's memories are tinged with the same nostalgia for an old order ("Petersburg is a European city that arose in Russia by miracle") swept away by violence. As for his childhood, it ended when he began boarding at the Imperial Theater School, where he lived in bare, comfortless quarters and spent his days immersed in a dancer's monastic discipline. Not long afterward, the rest of the Balanchivadze family left St. Petersburg and retreated to the Finnish *dacha* Meliton had bought with part of his winnings, leaving Georgi behind. They moved to Georgia in 1917. He never saw his mother or sister again.

Some who knew Balanchine well believed that the emotional scars left by this separation made it all but impossible for him to have normal relationships. "I think, perhaps, he had not learned in those days how to love another human being," Alexandra Danilova speculated. "Perhaps if he had not been separated so much from his family, he might have learned that—and learned not to bury his feelings." Might his "aristocratic" reserve have been the result of childhood sorrow? Georgi's fellow students all remembered him as quiet and withdrawn to the point of detachment. "Others would talk about their families," Danilova said, "but he did not." Certainly he found it hard to adjust to life at the Theater School, from which he claimed to have run away as soon as he got there. In old age, he described his school days with revealing harshness:

On Sundays my aunt sometimes came over and picked me up at school and took me home for the day. She lived in Petersburg.... [O]n Saturday the school was deserted, for two days. It was sad and lonely to be left. You'd go to church and stand there for some time. The school had a chapel. The master would be there with maybe two or three other students. You had to kill time before dinner. I would go to the reception hall and play the piano. There was no one there, total emptiness.

No amateur psychologizing is needed to imagine the effect such loneliness must have had on a sensitive young boy. Nor does it seem at all coincidental that Georgi developed a facial tic, a reflexive sniff that led his fellow students to nickname him "Rat." Most childhood tics are short-lived, but Balanchine's, like his impenetrable reserve, stayed with him for the rest of his life. "An intriguing twitch sometimes wrinkles his nose," Paul Taylor wrote after meeting him forty years later. "It's as if he's been exposed to too many *Nutcracker* mice."

Many a lonely child has found comfort in art, and Georgi was no exception. He was well on his way to becoming a fine pianist, and if at first he was bored to distraction by the repetitive routine of his ballet classes, he came to see their point when he took part in a performance of *Sleeping Beauty* at the Maryinsky Theater:

> I was Cupid, a tiny Cupid. It was Petipa's choreography. I was set down on a golden cage. And suddenly everything opened! A crowd of people, an elegant audience. And the Maryinsky Theater all light blue and gold! And suddenly the orchestra started playing. I sat on the cage in indescribable ecstasy enjoying it all—the music, the theater, and the fact that I was onstage. Thanks to *Sleeping Beauty* I fell in love with ballet.

After that he needed no more urging and quickly won recognition as one of the Theater School's most gifted students, frequently dancing small roles at the Maryinsky Theater. He would become a superb dancer, though he lacked the good looks and romantic appeal necessary to ensure a career as a *danseur noble,* ballet's equivalent of a leading man. Instead, Balanchine mainly danced character roles (his scintillating performance as Candy Cane in *The Nutcracker* was remembered by all who saw it). For now, though, he was still learning his craft, and his progress came to an abrupt halt in 1917, stopped dead by the October Revolution. The Theater School was closed by the Bolsheviks for more than a year, and Georgi moved in with his aunt. St. Petersburg, now renamed "Petrograd," degenerated into near chaos, while the boy whose life had already been disrupted beyond imagining now found himself scrambling to get enough to eat. "One time it was so bad, students were so hungry, we cooked dead cat from street and ate it," he said.

Once the Theater School and the Maryinsky (now renamed the State Theater of Opera and Ballet) reopened, Balanchine's life regained a measure of order, though his health was permanently affected by the years of revolutionary privation. He began studying music at the Petrograd Conservatory, became a full-time member of the State Ballet in 1921, and married a teenaged dancer, Tamara Geva, in 1922. She was the first in a long string of "muses" from whom he drew inspiration for his ballets, and it may be that she also inspired him to leap headlong into the artistic ferment of the moment. Czarist Russia had been isolated from the fast-spreading modern movement in the arts, nowhere more so than in the field of ballet. The story ballets created by Marius Petipa in the late nineteenth century, including the production of *Sleeping Beauty* that awakened young Georgi to the beauties of dance, had been preserved at the Maryinsky like flies in amber, just as the Theater School taught only the classical ballet techniques codified by Petipa and his contemporaries. Petipa's virtuosic yet refined choreography supplied the foundation for Balanchine's style, but by the time he joined the State Ballet, he longed for something more. He had started to experiment with choreography, and now he began making dances for Geva and a small group of friends that infused the classical vocabulary of Petipa with new ideas all his own.

Balanchine was not the only Russian choreographer to feel the tug of modernity. In 1909 Serge Diaghilev, an art connoisseur turned impresario, had organized a touring troupe of Russian ballet dancers whose performances were galvanizing European audiences. Though the Ballets Russes, as the company became known, never appeared in its native land, some of its dances were originally made for the State Ballet, including Michel Fokine's *Chopiniana* (known in the West as *Les Sylphides*), a plotless suite of dances set to the music of Chopin, among the first such works ever to be made. Balanchine took careful note of the way Fokine abstracted the fine-grained movements and balanced stage groupings of Petipa-style classical ballet from their original theatrical context, just as he learned from Fyodor Lopukhov's *Dance Symphony* (1923), a controversial "symphonic" ballet set to Beethoven's Fourth Symphony, in whose premiere he danced.

What set him apart, then and later, was his musical understanding. A pianist accomplished enough to play Chopin's technically demanding études, he had studied theory and composition and written unoriginal but competent pieces of his own.* For him, music and dance were in some fundamental sense the same thing:

---

*Balanchine let his piano technique slip in later life, but the solidity of his musicianship remained evident to fellow professionals. "When he sat down at the piano," said the violinist Nathan Milstein, one of his closest friends, "he didn't play so much as 'noodle,' blurring over the hard parts. But really, that didn't matter. Balanchine sight-read freely. And you could see immediately that he was a refined and responsive musician."

Music is something that occupies architecturally a
certain portion of time. In the dance, unless your
body fills time, occupies time, as music does, then
it means nothing. Gesture itself is meaningless. . . .
I had to try to paint or design time with bodies in
order to create a resemblance between the dance
and what was going on in sound.

This approach was different from that of any previous choreographer, even Petipa, whose dances were
set to commissioned scores painstakingly written to
order. Balanchine, by contrast, sought his inspiration in
the score itself rather than merely using it as a sound
track, an approach so original that Danilova believed it
to be the main reason why the State Ballet refused to
perform his work: "As a dancer, George was popular
and well-respected. . . . But as a choreographer, he had
no future there. His background was so unusual, with
the musical training he had acquired at the Conservatory, and his choreography was so innovative that he
began to seem threatening to our superiors."

Unwilling to conform, he persuaded some of his
dancer friends to join him in an experimental troupe,
the Young Ballet, which made its debut with a program
bearing the smile-making title "The Evolution of Ballet: From Petipa through Fokine to Balanchivadze." Almost none of his early choreography has survived, so it

is impossible to speak with any confidence about the dances he made for the group, though written accounts suggest that the best of them were more than merely promising. But the impoverished conditions under which they were made were anything but encouraging. Not only were Balanchine's memories of St. Petersburg too strong for him to settle for the gray drabness of Petrograd, but the combination of unheated theaters and inadequate meals was wrecking his already fragile health. In any case he suspected that the future of ballet was in the West. So was the composer whose music would help shape that future: Igor Stravinsky's scores for Fokine's *Firebird* and *Petrushka*, first performed at the State Theater a decade after their European premieres, must have had a staggering impact on the trained ear of a choreographer who was still making dances to the music of Rachmaninoff and Saint-Saëns. Even if he could not yet foresee the effects of Soviet totalitarianism on artistic freedom, he knew he had to leave Russia as soon as he could, if only to stay alive: "To go or not to go—I never had any doubts at all. None! I never doubted, I always knew: if I ever had the chance, I'd go!"

BY 1924 the Soviet Union was sending performers abroad on state-sponsored tours, and Balanchine was invited to put together a small ensemble to dance in

Germany. Geva and Danilova joined him, and the Soviet State Dancers made their slow way to Berlin by steamer and train. It was the first time any of them had had enough to eat in years. "We had forgotten what it felt like to be full," Danilova remembered. They danced in variety houses and beer gardens (and even, Geva later claimed, for the inmates of a madhouse), ignored a telegram ordering them to return home, went to London and played at the Empire Music Hall, then crossed the English Channel to Paris, where they ran out of work. Just as their money was running out as well, they received a telegram from Diaghilev. Would they care to audition for the Ballets Russes? They would, they did, and they were hired a week later.

Three-quarters of a century after his death, Serge Diaghilev remains one of the best-known names in ballet, though he never choreographed a single step, designed a single backdrop, or wrote a single note of music for the dance company with which he wrote himself into the history of art. Constant Lambert, who composed a score for him, wittily described some of the lesser lights who worked with the Ballets Russes as "merely the gunmen executing the commands of their Capone, who, like all great gangsters, never touched firearms himself." Perhaps he might better have been thought of as the counterpart of a great editor who, like the *New Yorker*'s Harold Ross, never wrote for his own magazine. In fact, Diaghilev had distinguished himself as the editor of *Mir Iskusstva* (World of Art), Russia's first real journal of the arts, and he approached the Ballets Russes in more or less the same way. Not for him the full-evening ballets on which his generation of dancegoers had been raised. Instead, he presented mixed bills of streamlined one-act stage spectacles that commingled the arts of choreography, music, and painting, thereby placing ballet at the epicenter of the modern movement. Cocteau, Debussy, Fokine, Matisse, Nijinsky, Picasso, Prokofiev, Ravel, Satie, Stravinsky: each of these men worked for Diaghilev at one time or another, and though their contributions were always identifiably personal, the collective results bore his own outsized stamp. Vain and snobbish, arrogant and high-handed, he ran the Ballets Russes like a plantation. Even Stravinsky, himself possessed of a Diaghilevan ego, unhesitatingly admitted that "Diaghilev was more strong-willed than all his artists. . . . [H]e controlled every detail of every ballet he produced."

A great editor is a talent scout first and foremost, and Georgi Balanchivadze's reputation had preceded him. Word of his work for the Young Ballet had gotten back to Diaghilev, who was always on the lookout for the latest thing, whatever it might be. The impresario hired Georgi as a dancer, but a studio run-through of *Marche funèbre,* set to the third movement of Chopin's Second Piano Sonata, persuaded Diaghilev that the young man was an unpolished gem. Within weeks

Georgi was throwing together ballet divertissements for the Opéra de Monte-Carlo, where the Ballets Russes danced in the off-season to pay its bills. In March of 1925 he made the dances for *L'Enfant et les sortilèges*, an opera-ballet with music by Ravel and words by Colette, and that summer he rechoreographed Diaghilev's revival of the Stravinsky-Matisse *Chant du rossignol*. He even had a new, Westernized name: Diaghilev dubbed him "George Balanchin." (The French-style terminal *e* would be added later, along with a similarly French *s* briefly appended to the end of his first name.)

A lesser man might have had his head turned, but Balanchine remained unimpressed, to some extent out of ignorance—he did not yet know enough about European modernism to gauge the significance of his new colleagues—but also because he was all too aware of the technical shortcomings of the postwar Ballets Russes, whose dancers were mostly an undistinguished lot. He was further insulated from the company's crosscurrents by his heterosexuality, which was so unswerving that the openly gay Diaghilev accused him of taking "a morbid interest in women." Balanchine returned the compliment a half century later, with interest:

> Nobody will believe me of course, but Diaghilev did not know anything about dancing. His real interest in ballet was sexual. He could not bear the

sight of Danilova and would say to me, "Her tits make me want to vomit." Once when I was standing next to him at a rehearsal for *Apollo*, he said, "How beautiful." I agreed, thinking that he was referring to the music, but he quickly corrected me: "No, no. I mean [Serge] Lifar's ass; it is like a rose."

It's impossible to know whether Balanchine painted that particular lily, but it was no secret that the leader of Europe's best-known dance company used his position to promote his male lovers, starting with Vaslav Nijinsky and very much including Lifar, who created the title roles in Balanchine's *Apollo* and *Prodigal Son*. In Tamara Geva's words, "Diaghilev always mixed his emotionalism, his personal life, with the person he promoted." Balanchine had no interest in that kind of backstage affair (though he would later do the same thing with any number of talented ballerinas in the making). He was married to Geva, and when their passion cooled, he took up with Alexandra Danilova, with whom he lived for several years.* "The first time I got married,

---

*"No one ever knew whether Georges and Choura [Danilova] were married," Nathan Milstein wrote. They weren't, though many of their friends and colleagues—as well as many journalists who wrote about Balanchine in later years—assumed otherwise.

I was young, I didn't care in the least," he said. "Married . . . so we're married. Then we both went abroad. And there, you look around, and there are so many marvelous women. . . . And then I thought, time to end all this." So resolute a womanizer could never be a true protégé of Diaghilev, and their relationship remained cordial but businesslike.

The unknown choreographer learned all he could from the famous connoisseur. Just as he had with Nijinsky and Léonide Massine, Diaghilev made Balanchine look at paintings and sculpture, determined to educate his new choreographer's eye, and laughed at his old-fashioned tastes in music, curtly informing him that Rachmaninoff was passé: "Diaghilev told me, 'My dear fellow, *golubchik,* don't be silly, it's terrible music! There are many wonderful composers in the world, but Rachmaninoff isn't one of them.'" But while Balanchine took the older man's advice seriously, he never accepted it uncritically. "You are very sure of yourself," Diaghilev told him at their first meeting. So he was. From the start of their collaboration, Balanchine had sensed that dance was the weak link in the Diaghilevan synthesis of the three arts: Fokine's once-innovative choreography for the Ballets Russes now looked quaint, while Massine's ballets made no impression on him at all. "Diaghilev was a real connoisseur, that I can say with certainty," he later remarked. "Especially since in those days there wasn't very much to understand in ballet, it was a quite simple thing." Even in those far-off days, he was his own man, open to influence but sure of himself and his gifts.

For now, though, he was content to work within the strict limits set by his mentor, turning out a string of dances whose trendy decor and light, undistinguished scores bore out Constant Lambert's brutal quip about Diaghilev: "Before the war he created a vogue for the Russian ballet, but after the war he merely created a vogue for vogue." A knee injury had forced Balanchine to give up most of his onstage roles, and his lack of interest in the pleasures of Parisian society kept him still further from the limelight. (It didn't help that the members of the Ballets Russes were mercilessly underpaid. "We made very little working for Diaghilev," he later said, "and spent those miserable sums on food.") Had Balanchine died in 1927, he would now be nothing more than a footnote to the gaudy tale of the Ballets Russes. A year later he made *Apollo,* and became immortal.

IGOR STRAVINSKY was the only classical composer of the twentieth century who was also a media idol. It took biographers and historians a long time to pry off the mask of celebrity and see him as he was: jealous, resentful, controlling, stingy to the point of miserliness, and sufficiently charming that his friends were usually willing to overlook his less attractive traits. It helped, of course, that he was the composer of *Firebird, Petrushka,* and *The Rite of Spring*—all written for Serge Diaghilev. Stravinsky loved ballet passionately, and in a way he also loved Diaghilev, but he loathed being under his thumb, much less knowing that it was Diaghilev who had made him famous, and they quarreled constantly. What he needed was a collaborator who would be to him what he was to Diaghilev: a junior partner, gifted in his own right but nonetheless prepared to subordinate himself to the composer's iron will.

Stravinsky met Balanchine during rehearsals for *Le Chant du rossignol.* Though little is known of their first encounter, he must have recognized at once that Diaghilev's new choreographer understood music not merely as a listener but as a trained practitioner. The distinction mattered to Stravinsky, who felt that Nijinsky's choreography for *The Rite of Spring* had been defective precisely because of its lack of musical sophistication:

> He believed that the choreography should re-emphasize the musical beat and pattern through constant co-ordination. In effect, this restricted the dance to rhythmic duplication of the music and made of it an imitation. Choreography, as I con-

ceive it, must realize its own form, one indepen-
dent of the musical form though measured to the
musical unit. Its construction will be based on
whatever correspondences the choreographer may
invent, but it must not seek merely to duplicate the
line and beat of the music. I do not see how one
can be a choreographer unless, like Balanchine,
one is a musician first.

Whether or not one agrees with Stravinsky's narrow
conception of the choreographer as musician, there can
be no doubt that Balanchine filled the bill to perfection—there had never been a more musically knowledgeable choreographer in the entire history of ballet—and the fact that he was twenty years younger
than Stravinsky must have made him all the more attractive. As for Balanchine, he could scarcely have been
blind to the advantages of working with the world's
most famous composer, though there was more to it
than that. Stravinsky's bumpily asymmetrical rhythms
and crisp timbres excited his kinesthetic sense. "I liked
his music," he said, "and I felt how it should be put into
movement." He felt something else, too. Asked by an interviewer to give his "first impression" of the composer,
he replied, "First of all, I had great respect for him; he
was like my father, since he was more than twenty years

older than I." In time they would become true friends, but everyone who saw them together in later life agreed that Balanchine treated Stravinsky with filial deference. According to Maria Tallchief, "George seemed to respect him more than anyone else in the world."

Their partnership began in 1928. Elizabeth Sprague Coolidge, one of America's great patronesses of music, had commissioned a one-act ballet from Stravinsky for performance at the Library of Congress in Washington, and he responded with *Apollon Musagète* (Apollo, Leader of the Muses), now known simply as *Apollo.* The half-hour piece was premiered in Washington in April with choreography by Adolph Bolm, but Stravinsky had offered the European premiere to Diaghilev, who produced it six weeks later in Paris. The critics were puzzled by the mellifluous score, while Balanchine's choreography, which combined Petipa-derived steps with odd poses and gestures that seemed at first glance anything but classical, left them cold. "It used to be said that the Russian Ballet would not be much without Stravinsky; his latest production makes us fear that soon it will not be much with him," wrote the anonymous reviewer of the London *Times,* the first of many times that staid publication would turn up its nose at Balanchine.

Most of what Balanchine later "said" about *Apollo* was filtered through the pens of ghostwriters, but his

best-known statement, suspiciously polished though it
sounds, has the ring of truth:

> I look back upon the ballet as the turning point in
> my life. In its discipline and restraint, in its sus-
> tained oneness of tone and feeling, the score was a
> revelation. It seemed to tell me that I could, for the
> first time, dare not use all my ideas; that I, too,
> could eliminate. I began to see how I could clarify,
> by limiting, by reducing what seemed to be myriad
> possibilities to the one possibility that is inevitable.

Typically, he starts with the music—and with good
reason. *Apollo* is one of the highlights of Stravinsky's
middle period, a luminous tribute to the neoclassical
ideal, at once unequivocally modern and brimming with
Tchaikovskyan lyricism. Though Diaghilev was later to
develop mixed feelings about the score (he actually cut
Terpsichore's variation in a few performances, until
Stravinsky found out and complained), he summed it up
well in a letter to Lifar: "It is, of course, an amazing work,
extraordinarily calm, and with greater clarity than anything he has so far done; and filigree counterpoint round
transparent, clear-cut themes, all in the major key; somehow music not of this world, but from somewhere above."

In his previous works for the Ballets Russes, Balanchine had been expected to work with one eye on the

box office. Now Stravinsky had given him a score of the utmost distinction, written by a man who understood ballet almost as completely as he understood music. Diaghilev told a friend that Balanchine's choreography was "pure classicism, such as we have not seen since Petipa's." In fact, it went well beyond that. Other ballet choreographers were experimenting with "modern" movement in the twenties, most notably Bronislava Nijinska in the version of Stravinsky's *Les Noces* that she choreographed for the Ballets Russes in 1923, but only Balanchine went beyond mere dabbling. At last Diaghilev had found a choreographer capable of making dances whose steps were as contemporary as their scores and decor.

Apollo is a portrait of the Greek god of song and music, danced by a cast of seven and accompanied by a small string orchestra. As the curtain rises, Leto gives birth to the young Apollo, who is freed from his swaddling clothes by two handmaidens. He takes up his lyre and plays, then dances about the stage, exploring his godly powers. He is joined by Calliope, the muse of poetry; Polyhymnia, the muse of mime; and Terpsichore, the muse of dance. Each dances a solo variation for Apollo, "instructing" him in her art. He dances with Terpsichore alone, then with all three muses. Having achieved his maturity, he then ascends Mount Parnassus to join Zeus, his father, in Olympus, followed by the muses, as Leto and her handmaidens bid him farewell from the earth below.*

Such is the "plot" of *Apollo,* and it is integral to understanding the dance, but the effect made by *Apollo* is nonetheless very different from that of a story ballet. While Apollo is a recognizable character who undergoes a transformation in the course of the work—he grows up—the point of the dance is not so much its vestigial plot as the encounters and events that occur throughout *Apollo,* and the subtle ways in which they arise from and relate to Stravinsky's score. At the end of her solo variation, Calliope scribbles a note in her hand with one finger, runs across the stage, and shows it to Apollo, who looks at it and abruptly turns away. In the Apollo-Terpsichore pas de deux, Terpsichore climbs atop the kneeling god's back, and the two stroke the air with their outstretched arms (a scene known to dancers as "the swimming lesson"). Later, Apollo and the muses

---

*In 1979 Balanchine eliminated the roles of Leto and the handmaidens, cut the birth scene, and rechoreographed the finale so that Apollo and the muses pose in a sunlit, peacocklike formation at center stage instead of ascending to Olympus. He apparently felt that the opening scenes had become dated and were out of keeping with the tone of the rest of the dance. ("I know why I changed it, I took out all the garbage—that's why!" he told an interviewer in 1981.) New York City Ballet now performs *Apollo* only in this shortened version, originally created for Mikhail Baryshnikov, but many other companies continue to dance the birth scene.

gallop together across the stage as if he were riding a chariot drawn by three horses.

Some of these occurrences are explicitly picturesque—at one point, Apollo and Terpsichore touch forefingers in a gesture borrowed by Balanchine from Michelangelo's *Creation of Adam*—while others border on the fully abstract. All are charged with multiple meanings that cannot be expressed in words, and Balanchine never attempted to explain what they meant. "I don't put meanings to any of my gestures," he said, though on occasion he might tell a dancer what had inspired them. Edward Villella described one such occasion:

> "This gesture, the open and closing of the hands when one of Apollo's arms is behind his back and the other is above his head—where did it come from?" I wanted to know. . . . He explained, "You know, I was in Soviet Union, awful place, no color, no paint. Lousy. No light. I went first time to London to Piccadilly Circus. Saw for first time flashing lights." In Apollo's vibrant hand gestures Balanchine had recreated his youthful impression of those glittering neon signs. To me they seemed like twinkling stars.

To an eye conditioned by a century's worth of modernism, such occurrences now seem natural enough (though they have lost none of their mystery), just as we take for granted the once-shocking spectacle of ballet dancers shuffling on their heels and flexing their feet instead of pointing them. In 1928, though, they startled audiences accustomed to an older style of ballet, one that combined traditional steps with representational pantomime. B. H. Haggin, an American music critic who later became one of Balanchine's most fervent advocates, found them inexplicable when he saw *Apollo* in Paris in 1928, not having seen the Ballets Russes since it toured the United States twelve years before: "To my eyes, for which in 1928 ballet was what they had seen in 1916—Fokine's *Les Sylphides, Firebird, Carnaval, Petrushka,* Nijinsky's *Afternoon of a Faun*—these innovations and inventions that I saw for the first time were strange and baffling." In time, he came to view them as the very essence of the choreographer's art, dubbing them *fantaisie Balanchine.* Balanchine may have learned the art of simplification from Stravinsky's white-on-white score, but *Apollo,* for all the simplicity of its classically based steps, is filled to overflowing with such strokes of fantasy, scattered throughout the score with the generosity of youth.

At the same time, the choreography and score of *Apollo* share a serenity that reminds us that Balanchine and Stravinsky were both devoutly religious. Stravinsky was immersed in the writings of Jacques Maritain, a neo-Thomist philosopher with a serious interest in music, when he was composing *Apollo,* and if Balanchine's faith was less intellectual than instinctive, he was as true a believer. "I don't tell anyone," he said once, "but I go to church by myself." In the spacious, seemingly timeless undulations of the *apothéose* that accompanies the ascent of Apollo and the muses, it is hard not to hear—and see—what Balanchine found there, though one need not interpret his vision in a specifically religious way. *Apollo* can also be seen as an "argument" for the superiority of Apollonian neoclassicism over Dionysian expressionism, a prime example of what the art critic Clement Greenberg had in mind when he advocated "the development of a bland, large, balanced, Apollonian art in which passion does not fill in the gaps left by the faulty or omitted application of theory but takes off from where the most advanced theory stops, and in which an intense detachment informs all." He might have been thinking of *Apollo,* whose purity of means and spirit were best described by Edwin Denby:

> *Apollo* is [an] homage to the academic ballet tradition, and the first work in the contemporary classic style. . . . [I]t becomes progressively a more and more directly classic dance ballet, the melodious lines and lyric or forceful climaxes of which are effects of dance continuity, dance rhythm, and dance

architecture. And it leaves at the end, despite its innumerable incidental inventions, a sense of bold, open, effortless, and limpid grandeur. Nothing has looked unnatural, any more than anything in Mozart sounds unnatural.

Despite the lukewarm response of its original critics, as well as many of those to come, *Apollo* remained close to Balanchine's heart, and Stravinsky's as well. It was, the composer said, "far more important than people realize. I think of *Apollo* as something entirely new in my music." It is the earliest of Balanchine's ballets to survive in its entirety; the choreographer would stage it for each of the successive companies with which he worked, gradually paring away its costumes and scenery (the original decor by the French painter André Bauchant having long since been jettisoned and forgotten) and teaching each of his Apollos to be what he called a "poet of gesture." In time the rest of the world awakened to its beauties. New York City Ballet still dances *Apollo* regularly, as well as on such ceremonial occasions as the centenary of Balanchine's birth, and it is equally popular with other companies. Of the five dozen works premiered by the Ballets Russes, it is the one that best explains why there once was a time when the whole world of art seemed to revolve around Serge Diaghilev and his band of geniuses.

Apollo was sui generis, something new under the sun. *Prodigal Son,* by contrast, represented the quintessence of the Diaghilevan formula: a fusion of the three arts, ennobled by choreography superior to anything (other than *Apollo* and Nijinska's *Les Noces*) that had come before it. Otherwise, Balanchine's last project for the Ballets Russes was in most ways the mixture as before, though it, too, is one of his finest and most popular dances.

Whereas Stravinsky's music for *Apollo* came to Balanchine ready-made, the score to *Prodigal Son* was composed to order by Sergei Prokofiev to illustrate Boris Kochno's libretto, a streamlined, Russianized retelling of the biblical parable. Georges Rouault, whose expressionist paintings on religious themes were more admired in the twenties than they are today, supplied costume designs and two dark backdrops. The score was appealing, the decor handsome, but it was the junior partner whose contribution mattered most. In addition to a half-dozen unforgettable strokes of *fantaisie Balanchine* (many of them in the two-part pas de deux in which an ice-cold Siren seduces the Prodigal Son, wrapping her long legs around him like a pair of cobras), it gives us our first glimpse of Balanchine the storyteller, recounting with undimmed legibility the thrice-told tale of the arrogant young man who runs away from home, falls among thieves, is despoiled and left for dead, and crawls into the arms of his father to be forgiven. Every twist in the plot of *Prodigal Son* is clear to the unaided eye, every relationship obvious without recourse to the libretto, in part because of Balanchine's masterly use of gesture, in part because he knew the difference between what can be shown and what must be told. He later coined a pithy axiom known in the world of dance as Balanchine's Law: "There are no mothers-in-law in ballet. You know, how does the audience know the character is somebody's aunt in story unless she's wearing sign that says Aunt?"

Balanchine rarely spoke of *Prodigal Son* save with mild disdain, doubtless because it was so unabashedly Diaghilevan. Perhaps for the same reason, Diaghilev told him after the Paris premiere that it was the best thing he had ever done, and unlike *Apollo*, it was a success. Even the critics deigned to approve. "One feels that Balanchine is a serious artist," Richard Capell wrote in the London *Daily Mail*, "striving with much intelligence to make new expressive forms." But Prokofiev hated the ballet—he had expected something more conventional looking—and refused to give Balanchine a share of the royalties. Balanchine responded by never again choreographing a Prokofiev score, while *Prodigal Son* itself went unseen between 1929, the year of its premiere, and 1950, when Balanchine revived it for New York City Ballet, casting Jerome Robbins in the title role. Francisco Moncion, Edward Villella, and Mikhail Baryshnikov followed Robbins, each making a similarly powerful impression on his generation of balletgoers. Its daringly explicit stage pictures have left their mark on countless other choreographers, and whenever Balanchine made a story ballet in later life, he drew on its narrative techniques. In addition, *Prodigal Son* is one of the few Diaghilev ballets that continues to be performed in something closely resembling its original form, not only by New York City Ballet but by other companies; Rouault's decor is always reproduced in modern revivals, and Balanchine made few ex post facto adjustments to his choreography. As a result, anyone wondering what it felt like to spend an evening at the Ballets Russes can find out simply by attending a performance.

Diaghilev saw *Prodigal Son* for the last time in London in July, having previously sent a letter to the *Times* in which he flamboyantly restated his credo: "For 25 years I have endeavoured to find a new *Mouvement* in the theatre. Society will have to recognize that my experiments, which appear dangerous today, become indispensable tomorrow. . . . I can picture to myself the bewilderment of the people who saw the first electric lamp, who heard the first word on the telephone." He then headed for the Continent, exhausted by the rigors of the season and the diabetes that was ravaging his plump body, making his way to Venice, the city he loved best, while his company followed him across the English Channel to give its final performance in Vichy. Afterward Balanchine returned to London to choreograph and perform in a dance sequence for a movie called *Dark Red Roses,* in which he plays a jealous Cossack. (The film survives, the oldest-known motion-picture record of Balanchine's choreography and one of the few documents of his dancing.) During the shooting, Anton Dolin, another Ballets Russes dancer who appeared in the film, picked up a newspaper and saw a picture of Diaghilev on the front page. He had died in Venice. His company collapsed under a mountain of unpaid bills and never performed again.

In years to come Balanchine spoke respectfully of his mentor, at least for public consumption. "It is because of Diaghilev that I am whatever I am today," he said, which was—up to a point—nothing more than the truth. The Ballets Russes had given him his first chance at fame, and he repaid it with *Apollo* and *Prodigal Son,* as well as other, lesser efforts that died with the company. Diaghilev teamed him with Stravinsky, introduced him to a new world of artistic possibility, gave him access to a troupe of dancers on which he honed his unformed style, and taught him how to oversee all the myriad activities of a ballet company. If what he did with that knowledge departed from the gospel according to Serge Diaghilev, it was because he had a different understanding of what ballet should be, one that needed no meddling impresario to call into being. Not for him the fizzy displays of chic that dazzled the public for a season or two but left behind only painted flats, tattered costumes, and fast-fading memories. Balanchine had ideas of his own, and though it would take him two decades to bring them to fruition—not in Europe, but in a new world he had seen only in his imagination—he knew how to wait.

3 · TOUGH POTATO

....

*A*CHOREOGRAPHER without dancers is like a carpenter without wood. Balanchine's work for the Ballets Russes had brought him little fame and less money. Only a handful of critics had known the radical innovations of *Apollo* for what they were. Yet in order to build on them, he would have to find another forward-looking ballet company prepared to take a chance on him—or start one of his own.

At one point it seemed possible, even likely, that the Paris Opéra would hire him to be its ballet master. The job would have been all but impossible, ballet at the Opéra having been in decline for decades, but Balanchine was invited to choreograph Beethoven's *Creatures of Prometheus* for the company in the fall of 1929, and lacking any more promising offers, he accepted, hoping for the best. Two weeks after reporting for work, he came down with pneumonia. His condition became dire—years of privation in Russia had weakened his lungs permanently—so he turned over the job of choreographing *The Creatures of Prometheus* to Serge Lifar, giving advice from his sickbed. Then the doctors discovered that he was also suffering from tuberculosis and rushed him to a Swiss sanatorium. "My life here is not gay," he wrote to Kochno a few weeks later, "and the only good thing about it is my hope." Upon his release, he learned that the unscrupulous Lifar had connived to secure the Paris Opéra job for himself.

Balanchine had nothing to say about Lifar's betrayal, then or later. Having come so close to death at so young an age, he determined instead to spend the rest of his days living in the present. It was a resolution from which he never wavered. Of all his oft-repeated refrains, the most familiar was *Do it now!* "Why are you stingy with yourselves?" he would ask his dancers. "Why are you holding back? What are you saving for—for another time? There are no other times. There is only now. Right now." His ruthlessly practical approach to running a dance company was rooted in the hard-won knowledge that his next breath might be his last. He worked within the means available at the moment, using them to the fullest, never wasting time longing for better dancers or a bigger budget: "A dog is going to remain a dog, even if you want to have a cat; you're not going to have a cat, so you better take care of the dog because that's what you're going to have." He ran his private life along the same lines: when he had money, he spent it lavishly, on himself and others, and when he didn't, he lived frugally. "You know," he said, "I am really a dead man. I was supposed to die and I didn't, and so now everything I do is second chance. That is why I enjoy every day. I don't look back. I don't look forward. Only now." *This* dance, *this* meal, *this* woman: that was his world.

Unable to make dances for a ballet company, he went to London and made them instead for Charles Cochran, whose lavish West End revues had already put Noël Coward on the theatrical map. From there he traveled to Copenhagen to stage six Diaghilev ballets for the Royal Danish Ballet. Two were by him, the other four by Fokine and Massine (though he changed them to suit himself). Next he spent a season as ballet master of the Ballets Russes de Monte-Carlo, a new company pieced together out of the ruins of the original Ballets Russes, whose stars, Irina Baronova, Tamara Toumanova, and Tatiana Riabouchinska, were twelve, thirteen, and fourteen years old. The press called them the "baby ballerinas," and Balanchine preferred their dancing to that of Danilova, whom he passed over for the new company. She had already left him, suspecting that his interest in her, both as a woman and as a dancer, was waning: "Sooner or later, George would have left me. Balanchine was like a painter who, over the length of his career, has several models, and he falls in love with each of them; his models are his inspiration and his passion. For George, his ballets depended on the women in his life."

They also depended on the circumstances of his life. He would never pass up an opportunity to make dances, be they for West End revues or Hollywood musicals. Wherever he worked, he gave of his very best. But he knew that without artistic control and the money to back it up, his creative vision would be compromised, and that was what happened now. In 1932 the Ballets Russes de Monte-Carlo replaced him with Massine—the ultimate insult—while his subsequent attempt to launch a Paris-based troupe, Les Ballets 1933, foundered after one short, financially unsuccessful season, now remembered only for the premiere of *The Seven Deadly Sins,* an intriguing hybrid of song and dance set in America and danced to the jazz-influenced music of Kurt Weill.

Like most Russians of his generation, Balanchine was interested in America, though he had never been there and his notions of it were approximate at best:

Russians always want to see America. We read about cowboys and Indians in our childhood. I read

Mayne Reid's *Headless Horseman,* and Cooper's *Last of the Mohicans.* We boys liked to play Indian. Chekhov has a story of how some schoolboys plan to run away to America and what happens. Then, of course, there were American movies: William Hart, Douglas Fairbanks, who leapt dashingly from a bridge onto a moving train or fearlessly climbed a rope over a chasm. Life in America, I thought, would be fun. . . . So many beautiful girls. Healthy girls—good food, probably. A country that had all those beautiful girls would be a good place for ballet.

Yet it had never occurred to him that he might actually live and work there—not until he made the acquaintance of a twenty-six-year-old American in Paris who talked him into coming to the New World to chase a dream that more reasonable men would have dismissed as half-baked.

MORE OFTEN THAN NOT, the first word that people who knew Lincoln Kirstein use to describe him is "crazy." Christopher Isherwood said he looked like "a mad clipper captain out of Melville." At the very least, he was unusually eccentric, and the violence of his enthusiasms, which ranged from classical ballet to Catholicism (to which he converted late in life), was surpassed only by the manic energy with which he espoused them.

Born in 1907, Kirstein was the second child of a wealthy family of Boston Jews who made their money in the department-store business. His six-foot-two frame, flinty Brahmin profile, close-cropped hair, wire-framed glasses, and sober black suits—silk in summer, wool in winter—served as camouflage for his unconventional cultural interests.* Not talented enough to make his mark as a painter or novelist, he tried his hand at editing, launching an influential quarterly called *Hound & Horn* while an undergraduate at Harvard, but he entertained delusions of greater grandeur, and by 1933 they had come into focus. In common with so many other homosexual aesthetes who were young in the twenties, he had fallen in love with dance after seeing the Ballets Russes and conceived the notion of starting a ballet company that would serve as an incubator for American modernism, much as Diaghilev had opened the eyes of countless Europeans to the modern movement in art. He meant to do as Diaghilev did,

---

*Most of the time, anyway. "A military buff, he sometimes dressed in khaki shorts and matching shirt as if he were a colonel in the British raj," wrote Maria Tallchief. "Other times he'd wear white shoes that clashed with the black suit he invariably had on."

serving as the company's creative spark plug and bringing together choreographers, composers, and visual
artists to create a synthesis of the three arts that was
uniquely American in tone, and he had enough money
to pursue his dream, though not enough to single-
handedly bankroll it. "I've had more trouble over money
than I've had over sex," he would ruefully confess.

Like Chick Austin and Virgil Thomson, two other
gay Harvard alumni who became key figures in American culture between the wars, Kirstein's point of view
was more Franco-Russian than Austro-German. He
also shared with them the same campy streak that led
Thomson to collaborate with Gertrude Stein on the
Dada-flavored opera *Four Saints in Three Acts*, which
premiered at the Wadsworth Atheneum, the Connecti-
cut museum run by Austin. But Kirstein, unlike his
friends, never fully understood or appreciated main-
stream modernism, praising such minor painters as
Paul Cadmus (his future brother-in-law) and Pavel
Tchelitchev (the voluble neoromantic who wrote the
book and designed the decor for *L'Errante*, one of Balanchine's Les Ballets 1933 productions) at the expense
of Matisse and Léger, whom he attacked as practition-
ers of "an amusement manipulated by interior decora-
tors and high pressure salesmen." Though a few of his
passions have stood the test of time—he wrote with

discernment about the photographers Henri Cartier-Bresson and Walker Evans and the sculptor Elie Nadelman—Kirstein would exert no substantial influence on the visual arts, either as a critic or as a patron.

In dance his instincts were surer. He went to Paris in 1933 to look for a suitable choreographer, having first prepared himself by taking dance lessons from Michel Fokine, a spectacle for which more than a few balletomanes would gladly have bought a ticket. ("How can Kirstein be a director of a ballet company?" Fokine later asked. "He took some ballet lessons from me, and he can't get his feet off the floor.") Five weeks later he met George Balanchine, and his diary entry recording their conversation has survived:

> He said one must not revive anything, ever; dancing, a breath, a memory; dancers are butterflies; the older ballets served their time; would look hopelessly old-fashioned now. How [Fokine's] *Schéhérazade* is now merely a bad joke, and his own *Fils Prodigue* would seem as bad. . . . He would like to come to America with twenty girls and five men, in a repertory of classical ballet in his own extended academic "modern" style. American students he has seen in Paris have great potential; very fast on their feet, but often dead from the waist up; they have spirit and can be touched into

fire. . . . Balanchine seemed intense, concentrated, disinterested; not desperate exactly, but without any hope.

Within days Kirstein had fired off a breathless sixteen-page letter to Chick Austin ("My pen burns my hand as I write: words will not flow into the ink fast enough") in which he outlined his plan to launch a Hartford-based ballet school and dance company run by Balanchine and operating under the auspices of the Wadsworth Atheneum. Like all of his schemes, this one was a volatile blend of hardheaded practicality and dilettantism run amok: "This school can be the basis of a national culture as intense as the great Russian Renaissance of Diaghilev. . . . It will mean a life work to all of us, incredible power in a few years." The school, he explained, would provide the necessary cash flow and supply the company with dancers trained in Balanchine's methods, who within a few years could perform a repertoire of new ballets on American themes. Needless to say, these ballets would be staged by Balanchine but masterminded by Kirstein, who obligingly sketched out a few of his ideas: "*Uncle Tom's Cabin:* ballet au grand serieux avec apotheose: by E. E. *Cummings.* He is doing it now on my suggestion. Music by Stephen Foster. . . . *Custer's Last Stand:* After Currier and Ives, the circling Indians: corps de ballet shooting at the chief dancers in the center." All it would take, he promised, was $6,000 to bring Balanchine and a few like-minded colleagues to America.

It's easy enough in retrospect to make fun of Kirstein's naive fantasies. It would have been easier in 1933, when American ballet was all but nonexistent. As for Balanchine, one can scarcely imagine what he made of the awkward, bespectacled giant who urged him to pull up stakes, move to a country he knew only from books, and start choreographing ballets about Uncle Tom and General Custer. But he had nothing better to do, so he agreed to give it a try. Chick Austin raised the money, and Balanchine duly sailed for New York in October. A few adjustments to Kirstein's plan soon proved necessary—Balanchine found Hartford too provincial, insisting that Manhattan was the only acceptable place for his base of operations—but three months later the School of American Ballet opened for business on Madison Avenue, and on June 10, 1934, its students gave the premiere of *Serenade*, the first Balanchine ballet to be made in America, set to Tchaikovsky's Serenade in C Major for Strings.

Photographs of that invitation-only performance exist, and they are at once touching and comical. It was given on a makeshift wooden stage erected on the lawn of the country estate of Felix Warburg, a banker whose son, Edward M. M. Warburg, was Kirstein's chief financial backer. The dancers look overweight, almost chunky, by today's more rigorous standards, just as the dance itself only partly resembled the *Serenade* that later became the signature piece of New York City Ballet.* Balanchine had thrown it together in his deceptively casual manner. One day he had seventeen girls on hand, so he lined them up in two interlocking diamonds, the tableau with which the dance begins, and started making steps; a few days later a girl came late to rehearsal, and he made her tentative entry into the studio part of the first movement. But nothing he did was as casual as it looked. Tchaikovsky was his favorite romantic composer, and the Serenade in C Major was one of his favorite Tchaikovsky pieces. He had long wanted to use it as the score for a ballet. The moment had come at last, and he seized it.

Though *Serenade* was made for a specific purpose—to teach the dancers of the School of American Ballet how to move in classical style—it was no occasional piece. Now that it is familiar and beloved, one has to look closely to realize how original, even iconoclastic, it must have seemed to those who first saw it on the

---

*Balanchine initially choreographed only three of the score's four movements, adding the *Tema Russo* six years later, and he would revise the ballet's choreography off and on until 1970.

lawn of the Warburg estate in 1934. To begin with, *Serenade,* unlike *Apollo,* is entirely plotless. Edwin Denby, that most poetic of dance critics, found it all but impossible to describe when he first wrote about the ballet a decade after its premiere:

> *Serenade* is a kind of graduation exercise: the dancers seem to perform all the feats they have learned, both passages of dancing and passages of mime (or plastique). There is no story, though there seems to be a girl who meets a boy; he comes on with another girl and for a while all three are together; then, at the end, the first girl is left alone and given a sort of tragic little apotheosis.

Still, Denby managed to cut through to the most important thing about *Serenade,* which is that it is a dance *about* dance, about the beauty of pure movement. Though the soloists each have their moments of glory, what one remembers above all is the unceasing sweep of the corps, swirling atop Tchaikovsky's music like a flock of doves. It's as if the soul of a nineteenth-century story ballet had somehow been lifted out of its rigid framework of plot and decor and given a life of its own. Breathtakingly specific "scenes" emerge from the constant swirl of movement like episodes in a dream. A ballerina lies prone at center stage, surrounded by five ranks of women who lift and lower their arms in ritual fashion. What does it mean? No one knows, nor did Balanchine ever explain the "little apotheosis" of the elegy, in which a woman whose lover (if he is her lover) has been taken away by an angel (if she is an angel) is solemnly lifted into the air by a group of blue-clad boys and carried in a procession whose apparent destination is a bright light that might be heaven (or fame, or love). One can make up any number of "plots" for *Serenade*, all equally plausible sounding and none of which explains its impenetrable mysteries. No dance is more romantic—yet Balanchine has taken Petipa's tutus and Tchaikovsky's tunes and bent them to wholly modern ends. For all its emotional specificity, *Serenade* is ultimately as abstract as a symphony, rooted in recognizable human interaction yet inexplicable save on its own terms. Fokine had tried to do the same thing in *Les Sylphides*, but to compare that slow-moving succession of pretty poses to Balanchine's flashing, darting tone poem is like putting a unicycle up against a streamlined train. If anyone else had previously made such a ballet, it has not survived. Very likely George Balanchine was the first choreographer to do so, and he would spend the rest of his life exploring the implications of the modest little masterpiece he whipped up to show his students how to look like dancers.

John Martin, the dance critic of the *New York Times*, called *Serenade* "a serviceable rather than an inspired piece of work" when he saw its New York premiere the following year, the first of two decades' worth of muddle-headed reviews of Balanchine's early ballets. Martin had been raised on modern dance and believed that only an American-born choreographer such as Martha Graham could create a distinctively American style of dance. His obtuseness was an unintentional tribute to Kirstein's farsighted vision. Not only were there no American-born choreographers with anything remotely approaching Balanchine's technical know-how, but the maker of *Serenade* had fallen in love with America at first sight. The tall buildings, the long-limbed, milk-fed bodies, the hum and buzz of urban life: all these things were to be reflected in his dances. Even *Serenade* is as much about the unself-conscious grace of the American women on whom it was made (and with whom he promptly embarked on an endless string of torrid affairs) as it is about the Russian romanticism Balanchine imbibed from his earliest days as a student at the Imperial Theater School. That was his way: everything he saw went into his work. He told Ruthanna Boris, who danced in the premiere of *Serenade*, "You have to look everywhere, everything, all the time. Look at the grass in the concrete when it's broken, children and little dogs, and the ceiling and the roof. Your eyes is camera and your brain is a file cabinet."

Kirstein, too, must have been puzzled by *Serenade*, if in a different way. It was the first American ballet by his handpicked choreographer, yet it had no book, no plot, no elaborate decor, and the music was not a commissioned score but a familiar piece of classical music. What had Kirstein contributed? Nothing but his money, energy, and determination: Balanchine had more than enough ideas of his own. *Custer's Last Stand* would never make it off the drawing board. But instead of huffily taking his ideas (and money) elsewhere, Kirstein chose to follow rather than lead, putting his inchoate gifts for what might be called inspirational administration in the service of a genius. "I began to sense that somehow I was now fatally aligned with a commanding historical process," he wrote of those early days. If so, it was a process in which his strong personality would become almost completely submerged. "People have trouble figuring out who I am," he liked to quip. "They can't make out if I'm a P.R. man for the City Ballet, or if it was all some kind of accident, or if I'm just a rich boy who tagged along." In fact, he was something far more remarkable: an amateur who turned himself into a professional. Without Balanchine, he might have spent the rest of his days chasing his own tail. Without Kirstein, on the other hand, Balanchine's genius might never have been recognized. The two men would never be personally close, but their destinies would thereafter be entwined—on Balanchine's terms.

For a brief moment, Kirstein's grand design seemed to be taking shape on schedule. The School of American Ballet attracted talented students, including a number of trained professionals whom Balanchine and Kirstein used as the core of a performing group, reviving three of Balanchine's Les Ballets 1933 dances and adding *Serenade* and another new work called *Alma Mater*, a dance about college football dreamed up by Edward Warburg. (Fledgling dance troupes will do a great deal to please their patrons.) Kirstein contributed an aggressive essay-manifesto to the program:

> Can Americans make good ballet dancers? This is a question which is an equivalent to asking whether or not Americans make good violinists, good painters, good poets. Physically speaking, Americans make the best dancers in the world with the possible exception of the Russians.... The form is capable of being assimilated by everyone. America is not an exception. Just as the civic symphonic orchestras of America are among the most brilliant in the world, so does America offer the world the possibility of a great ballet.

Critical response was mixed, but the public was impressed, and Edward Johnson, the new general manager of the Metropolitan Opera Company, invited Balanchine and his dancers, now called the American Ballet, to supply ballets for the Met's productions. It must have seemed like a brilliant idea on paper—that, after all, was how the Ballets Russes had subsidized itself in the twenties—but neither Balanchine nor Kirstein suspected that the Met's management cared nothing about the way its chronically shabby productions looked, only how they sounded. The company's sets consisted mainly of decaying flats, while its staging rehearsals were sketchy at best. Big-name singers rarely deigned to attend them in any case, a policy that remained unchanged until Rudolf Bing took charge of the company in 1950.

Johnson's notion of inviting a serious choreographer to make the Met's ballets was thus doomed from the start, and Balanchine and his dancers spent the next three years marking time in the most squalid, inartistic conditions imaginable, though they did their best to brighten the Met's primitive productions. "His ballets became the only lively things in the operas," Warburg remembered. "They showed up the Met and were therefore resented." Johnson permitted Balanchine to direct one opera, a 1936 revival of Gluck's *Orpheus and Eurydice* surrealistically designed by Pavel Tchelitchev, but the choreographer's innovations—he relegated the singers to the pit and left all the onstage action to his dancers—enraged the Met's conservative subscribers. Olin Downes, the *New York Times'* music critic, called the results "the most inept and unhappy spectacle this writer has ever seen in the celebrated lyric theater. . . .

The dancers who postured and fidgeted through helped matters very little." The production was seen only twice, though in years to come Balanchine would return many times to the myth of the lover whose uncontrollable longing brings death to his beloved.

To make money and keep busy, Balanchine began working on Broadway in 1936, staging dances for the latest *Ziegfeld Follies* and choreographing *On Your Toes*, a musical about a dance company. Its centerpiece was "Slaughter on Tenth Avenue," in which Tamara Geva and Ray Bolger (later to become famous as the Scarecrow in *The Wizard of Oz*) played a nightclub stripper and a tap-dancing hoofer who run afoul of a trigger-happy gangster. He got on well with Richard Rodgers and Lorenz Hart, who wrote the songs, and the show was a hit.* For the next decade he would do two or three Broadway shows a year, earning what for him were huge sums of money and spending them heedlessly. Had he come along a few years later, after Rodgers and Oscar Hammerstein revolutionized the musical-comedy form by writing shows in which book and score were integrated into a unified whole, he might now be regarded as the first great Broadway choreographer. Bolger thought as much:

---

*It was also the first Broadway musical whose dances were billed in the program as "choreography," a credit on which Balanchine insisted.

What Broadway taught Balanchine I don't know. Perhaps it taught him something that was important in his life, that there are other things besides Bach, Beethoven, and Brahms. Some of these things come from America. When you look at his modern ballets, you can see that Balanchine loved, adored, and worshiped such things. Hoedowns would be wonderful things to Balanchine. . . . He also taught them a little something: that in the American musical you don't have to do kick, stomp, thump, turn, jump, turn, kick. You can *dance.* He opened up a whole new world for the American musical comedy stage.

But none of the shows on which Balanchine worked would have an enduring life in revival, and except for "Slaughter on Tenth Avenue," which was filmed in 1939 and which he restaged as a freestanding dance for New York City Ballet in 1968, none of his Broadway choreography has survived in other than fragmentary form. In any case, he had no desire to see his name in lights—at least not the lights of Broadway. It wasn't that he didn't enjoy working there, nor did he see himself as a great artist slumming for cash. He loved American popular music, and his admiration for Fred Astaire was boundless: "He is like Bach, who in his time had a great concentration of ability, essence, knowledge, a spread of music. Astaire has that same concentration of genius; there is so much of the dance in him that it has been distilled." It was simply that he knew his real gifts lay elsewhere. "I'm like a potato," he told Bernard Taper. "A potato is pretty tough. It can grow anywhere. But even a potato has a soil in which it grows best. My soil is ballet."

Knowing that Broadway could never satisfy him and that his relationship with the Metropolitan Opera was doomed, Balanchine persuaded Kirstein and War-burg to take one last shot at putting the American Ballet on the map. The result was a two-night Stravinsky Festival held at the Met in the spring of 1937 that featured two new dances and the American premiere of *Apollo*. *Le Baiser de la fée* had originally been composed in 1928 for a production choreographed by Nijinska, while *Jeu de cartes*, a "ballet in three deals" about a poker game, was set to a commissioned score by Stravinsky. It must have been a sensational evening—the Ballets Russes come back to life—but the reviews, as usual, were mixed, and nothing came of it. Though the American Ballet spent one more year at the Met, there would be no more Balanchine nights, and he and his dancers departed at the end of the following season. "I try to adapt myself to the Metropolitan . . . but no use," he told the press. "The tradition of the Metropolitan is bad ballet. My dances the critics and dowagers did not like. They were too good. So I think. What shall I do? I will try something worse, maybe they will like it." Even Kirstein seemed to be having second thoughts. "Transplanting ballet in this country," he wearily informed a *New Yorker* reporter, "is like trying to raise a palm tree in Dakota."

The American Ballet duly dissolved, and Balanchine learned that for him, the only alternative to bad ballet appeared to be no ballet. Unable to find a company interested in his work, he succumbed briefly to the lures of Hollywood, but that, too, proved hopeless: a planned collaboration with George Gershwin was derailed by the composer's death, and *The Goldwyn Follies* (1938), the film on which they were to have worked together, ended up a pleasant but incoherent hodgepodge. Balanchine worked on three more films, but none was in any way memorable save for his fleeting cameo as a conductor in *I Was an Adventuress* (1940).* Outside of his salary, the only thing of value he brought back from Hollywood was a new wife, a half-German, half-Norwegian dancer called Brigitta Hartwig who went

---

*Meanwhile, Kirstein launched Ballet Caravan, a short-lived touring ensemble that performed the dances on American themes in which he had been unable to interest Balanchine. The only work from its small repertory that continues to be performed is Eugene Loring's *Billy the Kid* (1938, music by Copland), which was taken up by Ballet Theatre in 1940.

by the exotic stage name of Vera Zorina. No sooner did they meet on the set of *The Goldwyn Follies* than he began to court her. Following their return to New York, he made the dances for *I Married an Angel,* the show that turned Zorina into a Broadway star, and they married at the end of 1938.

Balanchine's second marriage, like his association with the Metropolitan Opera, made perfect sense—on paper. Zorina was beautiful and talented, while he already had a well-deserved reputation as a ladies' man. "Nobody escaped George," said Marie-Jeanne, his leading ballerina in the forties. "He had so many girls in the beginning. I think he went through all of them. It was just something you had to accept, that he was that fickle." But his previous entanglements had been with young dancers who longed to do his bidding on and off-stage, whereas Zorina was now famous in her own right and didn't care to be a ballerina, for Balanchine or anyone else: Broadway was good enough for her. Even if she had cared more about ballet, there was little he could do to help her, since the dance establishment had turned its back on him. Between 1937 and 1941 he made no ballets at all. In any case, Zorina did not return his all-consuming love. In her own tepid phrase, she saw him as "trustworthy and priestlike," unlike Orson Welles, with whom she had had a brief but intense involvement in the months just before her marriage, and though they remained married in name until 1946, she soon began seeing other men. "Balanchine was at the School one day during a difficult period with Zorina," said Natalie Molostwoff, who worked with him at the School of American Ballet. "We were suddenly ordered to leave the building because of a fire. We rounded up the dancers. Balanchine and I stayed until the last student left. He was cool, calm, and collected. 'I don't care,' he said. 'I just don't care now whether I live or not.'"

LONG AFTER Balanchine and Zorina had parted, he would observe, "Men tolerate pain or unhappiness worse than women: misfortune bends a woman—and it breaks a man." A weaker man might well have been broken by the combined effects of a marriage gone sour and a career gone flat. But work had always been his salvation, and at long last it started to come his way again.

First, the Ballet Russe de Monte Carlo, a new company led by Massine and unrelated to the Ballets Russes de Monte-Carlo, asked him to stage several of his ballets, including *Serenade*. A few months later the old Ballets Russes de Monte-Carlo, now known as the Original Ballet Russe, invited him to choreograph *Balustrade*, a new work set to the Stravinsky Violin Concerto.

Then, in 1941, the State Department asked Kirstein to put together a dance troupe to go on a goodwill tour of South America, and Balanchine supplied him with *Concerto Barocco* and *Ballet Imperial,* whose score was Tchaikovsky's little-known Second Piano Concerto.* Both were plotless, though totally different in style. *Barocco* was spare and spiritual (Suzanne Farrell has called it "eighteen minutes of salvation"), *Ballet Imperial* expansive and forthrightly romantic in tone, with a pas de deux in which a handsome young prince courts a ballerina who vanishes into a cloud of women, never to be seen again. Perhaps it is not too fanciful to find in this pas de deux a hint of Balanchine's thwarted love for Vera Zorina, though he himself would never have agreed with so reductive an explanation. To him, *Ballet Imperial* was "a contemporary tribute to Petipa. . . . It is a dance ballet and has no story." Be that as it may, the vain pursuit of an inaccessible woman would henceforth be the most frequently recurring "theme" in his plotless ballets. Jerome Robbins saw Balanchine's women as "elegant glamorous 'stars'—Garbo elevated, myste-

---

**Ballet Imperial was renamed *Tchaikovsky Piano Concerto No. 2* when Balanchine revised and restaged the ballet for New York City Ballet in 1973, eliminating the traditional Russian-palace scenery of the original 1941 production and bringing it more closely in line with his neoclassical style. (It is still commonly referred to as *Ballet Imperial* when performed with scenery.)

rious, provocative, extremely refined—a product of richness of taste and elegance." To dance with such creatures could be a daunting experience. "Partnering Balanchine's ballerinas," Edward Villella said,

> the cavalier is aware of the remoteness of the woman, but I also think there is a great deal of restraint and respect. . . . All of his pas de deux are similar. They are rarely overly romantic. There is always a sense of detachment and respect. There's always a touch of story. He leaves you with a theme and he allows you room to think.

Autobiographical or not, *Ballet Imperial* is self-evidently an homage to Petipa, and to Russian ballet in general. Like *Serenade,* it suggests a full-evening story ballet divested of its plot, leaving only the essentials of movement and mood, whereas *Concerto Barocco* harks back to the small scale and extreme concentration of *Apollo.* Though the ballets are rarely danced on the same program, they aptly sum up the two sides of Balanchine's artistic personality, and under more favorable circumstances they would undoubtedly have signaled the beginning of a period of renewed creativity. But since they were made for an ad hoc touring troupe, not a full-time company, Balanchine was in no position to follow them up, and in the next four years he managed to produce only five ballets, none of them memorable. Instead he spent his time and energy cranking out dances for second-rate Broadway shows, choreographing *Circus Polka,* a Stravinsky "ballet" for the elephants of the Ringling Bros. and Barnum & Bailey Circus, and doing whatever other well-paid piecework came his way.

Things improved when the Ballet Russe de Monte Carlo hired him in 1944 as its resident choreographer. Though he made only one work of lasting interest for the company—a Bellini ballet called *Night Shadow* (later renamed *La Sonnambula*) that gave Alexandra Danilova her most celebrated starring role—he was able to present carefully rehearsed performances of *Ballet Imperial, Barocco,* and *Serenade* in New York, where they were reviewed by Edwin Denby, now the regular dance critic of the *Herald Tribune.* Denby's praise of "the greatest choreographer of our time . . . Petipa's heir" offered for the first time a countervailing voice to the philistinism of the *New York Times.* Where John Martin saw in *Concerto Barocco* "sweet and superficial formalisms interspersed with acrobatics," Denby saw it as "the masterpiece of a master choreographer . . . everywhere transparent, fresh, graceful, and noble." Such advocacy, appearing as it did in one of New York's leading newspapers, helped alert a new generation of dancegoers to Balanchine's significance.

His foothold in the world of ballet remained precarious. In his first quarter century as a choreographer, he had made only six dances—*Apollo, Prodigal Son, Serenade, Concerto Barocco, Ballet Imperial,* and *La Sonnambula*—that continue to be performed today. If he was known to the public at large, it was for his work on Broadway, and several seasons had gone by since he was last associated with a full-fledged hit. As for his lucid neoclassicism, it struck many as old-fashioned, even quaint, by comparison with the high-strung "psychological" ballets of Antony Tudor, whose involuted plots and comparative sexual frankness made him the most talked-about choreographer of his generation. Agnes de Mille's *Rodeo,* a jovial cowboy ballet set to the all-American music of Aaron Copland, had been the biggest hit of 1942, while Jerome Robbins's *Fancy Free,* an Astaire-flavored sailor-suit dance with a raucously jazzy score by an up-and-coming young conductor named Leonard Bernstein, received two dozen curtain calls at its Metropolitan Opera House premiere in 1944.

Not coincidentally, Tudor, de Mille, and Robbins were all associated with Ballet Theatre (now American Ballet Theatre), the popular new company that dominated the dance scene in wartime New York. The ever-helpful John Martin explained in the *Times* that its repertory was not "created with the approval of Paris and the Riviera in mind," an unsubtle swipe at Balanchine. In fact, Lucia Chase, Ballet Theatre's director and chief patron, was willing, even eager, to make use of Balanchine, but only on her own terms: she intended to run things herself rather than ceding artistic control to any one choreographer, however talented. Balanchine staged *Apollo* and made *Theme and Variations* for Ballet Theatre, but his relationship with the company remained distant, then and later. He knew he needed a company of his own, and the Ballet Russe de Monte Carlo, which spent most of its time on the road, was a stopgap about which he had no illusions. Up to a point it had served him well, as had Broadway, but that point had been reached. Now he had to find a way to give up the frustrating life of a freelance choreographer, once and for all.

4 · THE VERY EXPENSIVE TREE

···

*W*ORLD WAR II passed Balanchine by. He had become an American citizen in 1939 but was too old to be drafted, and would have been rejected in any case because of his lungs. Kirstein, on the other hand, was just young enough to serve, and while his homosexuality would have disqualified him, he chose to conceal it. He spent the war in Europe, serving as a chauffeur for George Patton and, later, in the Monuments, Fine Arts, and Archives Division of Patton's Third Army. As soon as the war was over, he rushed back to New York to resume his partnership with Balanchine. It was high time, he thought, for the two men to take another stab at starting their own company:

> Through the spring and summer of 1946, Balanchine and I planned strategy. . . . Our proposals

were often reckless or, I suppose, "pretentious." That is, we would pretend to an impact which would be unprecedented in scope and quality. One thing we never considered was "success." There would be no compromise with good taste or establishment standards; to attach ourselves to these spelled death, as our experience with the Metropolitan Opera had proved. Balanchine and I knew that what had been done in the past had no place in a present or future. We needed fresh attitudes, new audiences, and our own theater; we set about obtaining these according to a rational schedule.

In October they announced the formation of a non-profit subscription-only "Ballet Society" dedicated to "the advancement of the lyric theatre by the production of new works . . . including ballet, ballet-opera, and chamber-opera, either commissioned by Ballet Society or unfamiliar to the American public." For $15 a year (about $145 today), members would receive single tickets to four productions. No individual tickets were sold—to attend one performance, you had to subscribe to the whole season—and no free tickets were given out to the press. "If newspapers cared to cover our performances," Kirstein explained, "they could subscribe, like anyone else. We calculated that, instead of antagonizing critics (who by and large would be unfriendly anyway), this might pique their curiosity, while they would scarcely ignore productions of such intrinsic interest." The first production was a double bill of *L'Enfant et les sortilèges,* the Ravel-Colette opera that Balanchine had staged for Diaghilev in 1925, and *The Four Temperaments,* a new ballet set to a score by Paul Hindemith for piano and strings, with decor by the surrealist painter Kurt Seligmann. Balanchine had commissioned the music from Hindemith in 1940, paying for it out of his Broadway earnings, but this was his first chance to put it onstage.

Only Kirstein would have dared to describe so lunatic an experiment in theatrical idealism as "rational," and in 1934 it would doubtless have sunk without a trace. But by 1946 New Yorkers were open to modernism as never before. Figurative painting was giving way to abstract expressionism, swing to bebop, and fluffy musicals to film noir. Truman Capote, Norman Mailer, and Flannery O'Connor were writing their first novels; *The Glass Menagerie* and *The Iceman Cometh* were playing on Broadway. Why not a subscription-only ballet company that made no pretense of pandering to the carriage trade? Eight hundred subscribers agreed, and their checks gave Kirstein enough working capital to get started. He booked the auditorium of the Central High School of Needle Trades, gave away the unsold seats to students and artists, and left the rest to his partner.

Balanchine had just parted company with Vera Zorina and proposed to Maria Tallchief, a dancer with the Ballet Russe de Monte Carlo whom he was in the process of turning into a world-class ballerina. Half Scots-Irish, half Osage Indian, Tallchief found her older suitor "everything a young girl could want—witty, debonair, handsome." He in turn saw her as the personification of America: the man who loved string ties and Western shoot-'em-ups had gotten himself a redskin bride to go with them. Free from his destructive obsession with Zorina, he was ready to create again. He married Tallchief on August 16, 1946, and three months later the curtain went up on Ballet Society.

It was by all accounts a near-run thing. The program featured a miscellany of dancers familiar with Balanchine's methods, ranging from Gisella Caccialanza and Elise Reiman, who had been in the very first *Serenade,* to Tanaquil Le Clercq, a seventeen-year-old student at the School of American Ballet. The auditorium was ugly, the stage perilously shallow, and there was no pit for the fifty-odd musicians. The stagehands were still hammering away at the set as the audience arrived, and the curtain went up a nerve-racking half-hour late. But *L'Enfant et les sortilèges* was bewitching, *The Four Temperaments* overwhelming, and though John Martin still seemed determined to resist Balanchine's genius (he saw "nothing very advanced" in *The Four Tempera-*

ments), most of the other critics echoed Edwin Denby, who declared the evening one of "startling brilliance," praising *The Four Temperaments* as "a novelty of extraordinary fascination and power.... [N]o choreography was ever more serious, more vigorous, more wide in scope or penetrating in imagination." Amused by Kirstein's decision not to invite the press, *Time* dubbed Ballet Society "Ballet Underground." Far more important than the magazine's typical condescension, though, was the fact that it had deigned to take note of the new venture. After a decade of frustrating false starts, Balanchine and Kirstein had hit the target.

Balanchine would restage *L'Enfant et les sortilèges* twice more, for New York City Ballet's Ravel Festival in 1975 and on PBS in 1981, but it was *The Four Temperaments* that made the more lasting impression. Like most of his dances, it is a plotless visualization of Hindemith's richly absorbing score, a three-part theme followed by four variations representing the "temperaments" of medieval physiology—melancholic, sanguinic, phlegmatic, and choleric—whose relative proportions in the body were thought to determine one's personality. Neither Hindemith nor Balanchine took the premise literally, using it as a pretext for the creation of four sharply contrasting theatrical moods. "Melancholic" shows us a man fighting against gravity, trying to break free but sinking helplessly to the stage, surrounded by a half-dozen goose-stepping women who thwart his will, then leave him alone in his mute anguish. "Sanguinic" is a waltz-time variation for a ballerina who dances with pinpoint exactitude, carried about the stage by her partner in a thrilling series of flying lifts. "Phlegmatic" is a droll soft shoe for a Ray Bolger–like hoofer flanked by four gorgeous chorus girls. "Choleric" opens with a cadenza in which a young woman hurtles from the wings as if fired from a cannon, darting this way and that. As she skitters about the stage, Balanchine reassembles the entire cast in a series of sleight-of-hand entrances leading to a finale in which the steps of the preceding theme and variations are rapidly reprised, flashing by like shooting stars. The corps then forms two horizontal files, a runway down which the women are carried in the flying lifts of "Sanguinic" as the curtain quickly falls, an awesome coup de théâtre that always brings down the house.

For Jerome Robbins, the climactic lifts suggested "some momentous departure—like interplanetary travelers taking their leave of the world." To me, it is as if I have beheld the working out of a fearsomely complex equation whose triumphant solution causes the universe to explode into being. Some see in "Melancholic" a portrait of the artist himself, reduced to despair by the women he idealized. In Arlene Croce's oft-quoted description, "The corps is a few small girls, a small menace. But they are enough to block and frustrate his every attempt to leap free. He leaps and crumples to earth. We recognize this man: his personal weather is always ceiling zero. (It's a nineteenth- rather than a seventeenth-century conception of melancholy—Young Werther rather than Robert Burton.)" All these explanations of *The Four Temperaments* have their merits, but none is necessary. Its visual metaphors, like those of *Serenade,* are sufficiently open to allow an infinite number of interpretations, while its style of movement—an amalgam of old-fashioned virtuosity, contemporary angularity, the gravitational pull of modern dance, and the off-center syncopation of jazz—is as fresh today as it was in 1946.

The only thing wrong with *The Four Temperaments* was the overcomplicated decor of Kurt Seligmann, who had been recommended to Balanchine by Tchelitchev. No one liked it, in part because the costumes obscured the dancers' bodies and hindered their freedom of movement. "Seligmann swathed our dancers in cerements, bandages, tubes, wraps, and tourniquets," Kirstein wrote, "so that dancing became more a dress parade than a display of human bodies in motion." Balanchine was reportedly snipping away pieces of the costumes right up to curtain time, but it would not be until 1951 that he disposed of them altogether, dressing the dancers in simple practice clothes and placing them in front of a sky-blue cyclorama. He had tried presenting *Concerto Barocco* in a similar manner as early as 1945, but the results were poorly received by critics who took for granted the Diaghilevan assumption that no ballet is complete without a set. Now that he had his own company, he could do as he pleased, and for the most part he would choose to present his plotless dances free of the costly distraction of Ballets Russes–style decor. For him, dance was about music and movement, and anything that obscured their relationship was superfluous. "When you get older, you eliminate things," he said. "You want to see things pure and clear."

Once *The Four Temperaments* was freed of its encumbering decor and made fully visible, it began to be performed by other companies and was soon recognized as a landmark work. When PBS invited New York City Ballet to appear on *Dance in America* in 1977, Balanchine chose it for the company's first broadcast. Twenty-three years later, *Time* called *The Four Temperaments* the greatest dance of the twentieth century, ranking it with such milestones of modernism as Matisse's *The Red Studio* and Stravinsky's Symphony of Psalms.

THE GREATEST DANCE of the century is by definition a hard act to follow, but Balanchine and Kirstein spent the next two seasons doing their best to oblige. By 1947 they had accumulated enough subscribers to move to City Center, a crumbling midtown theater owned by the city of New York that could be rented for $500 a night, no small consideration for a company that could only pay its dancers $18 a performance. (They rehearsed for free, and Balanchine drew no salary at all, living off his paltry performance royalties and his work for other companies and on Broadway.) The sight lines were ideal for dance, though the backstage facilities, one dancer recalled, were sordid: "There was some cooling for the audience, but upstairs in the dressing rooms air came only from open windows at the fire escapes. We endured peeping toms and burglars who stole our wallets when we were all onstage. Naked lightbulbs hung over the dressing room tables." It was there, in the spring of 1948, that Ballet Society premiered *Orpheus*, a subdued, lyrical retelling of the myth of Orpheus and Eurydice, set this time not to Gluck but a Stravinsky score commissioned by Kirstein, who paid $5,000 for the privilege. The symbolic decor was created by the sculptor Isamu Noguchi, whose collaborations with Martha Graham had made him one of the most admired stage designers of the forties, and Maria Tallchief danced the role of Eurydice. The first performance, conducted by the composer, was a rip-roaring success.

A few days later, Morton Baum, the hard-boiled tax lawyer who served as City Center's general manager, asked Kirstein to pay him a visit. "I am in the presence of genius," he had told the house manager after seeing a rehearsal of *Orpheus.* Now, to Kirstein's astonishment, he asked, "How would you like the idea of having Ballet Society become the New York City Ballet?" What Baum had in mind was for Ballet Society to serve as City Center's resident dance company, performing at a top price of $2.50 per ticket in return for in-kind subsidies that would cover some of its expenses. It was a risky proposition, and City Center's inadequacies were glaringly obvious, but Ballet Society's debts were mounting, and the arrangement would not only provide a much-needed cash poultice but give Balanchine and his dancers a home of their own. Kirstein took a deep breath and blurted out a promise as rash as Baum's offer: "I will give you in three years the finest ballet company in America."

New York City Ballet made its debut at City Center with *Concerto Barocco, Orpheus,* and *Symphony in C,* an exhilaratingly fizzy exercise in pure neoclassicism set to the music of Georges Bizet, the composer of *Carmen,* and conducted that night by Balanchine himself.* The

---

*"The tempo went like fire," recalled NYCB conductor Hugo Fiorato. "The dancers could hardly keep up with him. He knew, innately, what the tempo should be, probably better than anybody who ever lived. But when it came to doing it himself, he was so excited, so thrilled with having the orchestra, a whole new set of people to choreograph for! The dancers nearly went wild onstage. They couldn't help it. They just couldn't keep up with him. But it was marvelous. He conducted like an angel."

three works were already in its repertory—*Symphony in C* had been made the year before for the Paris Opéra—and thus could be revived quickly and cheaply. At first NYCB (the company's nickname) only danced on Mondays and Tuesdays before half-empty houses, but its association with Stravinsky gave it considerable cultural cachet, and it soon attracted influential admirers. One of them, B. H. Haggin, the music critic of the *Nation*, declared Balanchine to be "the greatest living creative artist." Other artists and writers started attending the company's modestly priced performances, assuring their friends that a modern master was in residence at City Center. "He's not an intellectual, he's something deeper, a man who understands everything," said W. H. Auden. In addition to Auden, his fans would eventually include Joseph Cornell, Marcel Duchamp, Edward Gorey (who attended virtually every NYCB performance between 1953 and 1983), Irving Howe, Willem de Kooning, Hilton Kramer, Robert Lowell, Marianne Moore, Frank O'Hara, and Susan Sontag.

But Balanchine knew that cachet, however gratifying, pays no bills. What he needed was a hot ticket that would fill City Center's 2,700 seats with people who knew nothing about dance, and he hit the bull's-eye in 1949 with *Firebird*, a Ballets Russes staple, starring Maria Tallchief in the title role and designed by none other than Marc Chagall. Morton Baum had bought Chagall's elaborate costumes and scenery from Sol

Hurok for $4,500 (they had originally been made for an unsuccessful Ballet Theatre production bankrolled by Hurok), and Balanchine shrewdly agreed to choreograph a new *Firebird* around them. Francis Mason, who saw the premiere, remembered it as a pivotal moment in the company's young life:

> When the curtain fell on that mighty processional of Stravinsky's, the audience rose to its feet and began the ovation every Balanchine advocate in America had been waiting fifteen years to hear. The cheering was so loud, it was as if we were in a football stadium instead of a theater. A man standing behind me in the mezzanine yelled at the top of his lungs over and over, "Tallchief! Tallchief! Tallchief!" When Maria Tallchief took her first solo bow, I thought the roof would cave in. . . . In the New York *Times* the next day, the dance critic John Martin said that Tallchief danced like a million dollars. On second thought, he said, like two million dollars. The box office was deluged.

Martin's belated conversion was no less pivotal. Only a year before, he had reviewed *Symphony in C* with his customary incomprehension: "Mr. Balanchine has once again given us that ballet of his, this time for some inscrutable reason to the Bizet Symphony." His sentiments were echoed by numerous critics and more than a few choreographers, for whom Balanchine's plotless, music-driven neoclassicism was an empty shell, all technique and no feeling. "George had only to go into his studio and put his step-step-steps together," Antony Tudor sneered. "Voila! A new ballet."* Now, with the dance critic of New York's most prestigious newspaper in his corner, Balanchine found himself in a much stronger position. The Sadler's Wells Ballet (now the Royal Ballet) invited him to come to London and stage *Ballet Imperial,* and after the first performance, which received seventeen curtain calls, David Webster, the company's general manager, invited NYCB to come to Covent Garden for a six-week summer season, followed by a tour of the provinces. "I can assure you London will make or break you," Webster said. The stakes weren't quite that high, but they were high enough: a triumphant tour of England would boost the company's prestige at home.

The London season went well enough, though it was far from a triumph. Balanchine brought eighteen ballets to Covent Garden, twelve by him and eight of

---

*In fact, Tudor thought much more highly of Balanchine than that, just as Balanchine admired Tudor's *Jardin aux Lilas* and *Romeo and Juliet,* but the two men were too different in temperament and sympathies to be friends.

them plotless, and most of the critics, in thrall to their memories of Diaghilev, responded tepidly. Cyril Beaumont, the critic of the *Sunday Times*, called Balanchine's choreography "cold" and "impersonal." Nor were Beaumont and his colleagues much impressed with the company's dancing, which struck them as haphazard and hyperathletic by comparison with the neat, well-drilled Sadler's Wells performances on which they doted. What they disliked was what Balanchine demanded. "Don't be polite!" he told his dancers over and over again. "No polite dancing. Polite is boring. We don't need that." He sought speed, drive, excitement, and risk, all of which he valued over the lifeless elegance of a classicism gone to seed. Suki Schorer, an NYCB dancer who would later teach at the School of American Ballet, remembered a rehearsal at which Balanchine drove home his point in an unexpected way:

> Mr. B stopped rehearsal and said to one of the dancers, "No! Not big enough, does not travel enough, feet come together too slowly in assemblé. Do again." The entrance was repeated, and the dancer put more effort and energy into the steps. Mr. B said, "Better, but not good enough." The dancer went back upstage, determined to give it everything. Putting every ounce of energy she had into each step as she came downstage, she came

flying through the air in a big assemblé with her feet together . . . and landed on her bottom, right in front of Mr. B. "That's right," he said with a smile, "now I see something."

That kind of daredevil energy was part and parcel of Balanchine's neoclassicism. "The New York City dancers," wrote Kirstein, "epitomize in their quirky legginess, liner accentuation, and athleticism a consciously thrown away, improvisational style which can be read as populist, vulgar, heartless, overacrobatic, unmannerly, or insolent." Most English critics found it unrefined.* One who thought otherwise was Richard Buckle, whose reviews for the London *Observer* sounded a diametrically opposed note: "The scantiness of scenery used by New York City Ballet is at first disappointing, but so much is expressed in Balanchine's choreography that in the end we feel more richly treated than ever before. . . . One thing that is clear about Balanchine's *Firebird,* which some of my matronly colleagues have been deploring, is that it is a great deal better than Fokine's. . . . Like a diver he plunges into the dark

---

*Balanchine in turn told his dancers that English dancing was "very proper, exactly right, and not very interesting." On a later tour he informed a well-known dance critic that in England, "if you are awake it is already vulgar."

depths of music and comes back quietly with a pearl." Four decades later Buckle would write a biography of Balanchine in which he said that "my life was changed by the revelation of [his] varied genius." Many English dancegoers were inclined to agree, and the London season, though it lost the company the fearful sum of $40,000 (nearly $300,000 today), was seen in New York as a giant step forward. "There is no doubt whatever," John Martin wrote in the *Times* on the company's return, "that the successful outcome of the young company's daring invasion of London's Covent Garden Opera House last summer has done wonders for its morale, and it has returned to its home stage in the finest of spirits raring to go."

IN LONDON Balanchine shared the spotlight with a younger man who also divided his time between ballet and Broadway, though the two had next to nothing else in common. Not only was Jerome Robbins more famous than George Balanchine in 1950, but he had become a celebrity while Balanchine was still struggling to put together a company of his own. The success of *Fancy Free,* made while Robbins was still a dancer with Ballet Theatre, freed him to pursue his own interests, and he choreographed three hit shows in quick succession, *On the Town, Billion Dollar Baby,* and *High Button Shoes.* Then he saw NYCB at City Center in 1948, and the experience changed his life as completely as it had Buckle's and Baum's. "Everyone was dancing so rapturously," Robbins recalled, "that I absolutely fell in love with it. . . . I thought, oh, boy! I want to work with that company! So I wrote [Balanchine] a note and said '. . . I'd like to work with you, I'll come as anything you need or anything you want. I can perform, I can choreograph, I can assist you.'—I got a note back saying 'Come on.'" He joined the company the following season, and a few months later was named associate artistic director.

From the outset, Robbins's story-driven one-act ballets proved an ideal foil for Balanchine's plotless dances, while his charismatic stage presence inspired Balanchine to feature him in *Bourrée Fantasque* (1949, music by Chabrier) and to revive *Prodigal Son* for him in 1950, the first time it had been danced since Diaghilev's death. At the same time, Balanchine must have known that Robbins would be hard to live with. A half-closeted homosexual (he became more open about his sexuality in later life) who had serious involvements with several women and found it hard to accept his stronger attraction to men, Robbins was notorious on Broadway for the bullying arrogance with which he tried to cover up his deep-seated insecurities. Balanchine made a point of treating him with unfailing respect, giving him first call on the company's dancers and rehearsal space and going out of his way to soothe the feelings of those over whom he ran roughshod. "Except in a few instances," NYCB's Richard Tanner recalled, "Balanchine always stood up for Jerry. When somebody was screaming, 'He's just impossible to work with, we can't,' or dancers were going into the office and saying, 'I just don't want to be in his ballets anymore,' Balanchine would calm them down, tell them that they didn't understand how good being in Jerry's ballets was for their careers, what they were learning, and the public perception of their dancing."

What Balanchine himself thought of those ballets is harder to know. "George was convinced that Jerry was the only choreographer besides himself who could be taken seriously," Betty Cage, the company's general administrator, said unequivocally. But the two men were never close, and many dancers, then and later, were no less sure that Balanchine regarded Robbins as a superficial crowd-pleaser. Arlene Croce described him as "fatally attracted to pretentious undertakings," a fair enough description of more than a few of his weaker efforts, and only four of the dances he made for New York City Ballet in the fifties, *The Cage* (1951, music by Stravinsky), *Afternoon of a Faun* (1953, music by Debussy), *Fanfare* (1953, music by Britten), and *The*

Concert (1956, music by Chopin), would enter the permanent repertory. Yet of all the choreographers of note who passed through City Ballet in that decade, Robbins was the only one who forged a lasting relationship with the company, and it is hard to imagine that Balanchine would have behaved so generously toward a colleague for whom he had no respect. Robbins in turn worshipped Balanchine, whom he called "the great master of our age," but he was also ferociously competitive, so much so that at least one City Ballet dancer, Jacques d'Amboise, later claimed that he had longed at one time to "take over the company." Their relationship was further complicated when—improbable as it sounds—both men found themselves in love with the same woman.

It was Balanchine's habit to fall in love not with creatures of flesh and blood but with fantasies of his own devising. Like most such romantic idealists, he was aroused by pursuit and disillusioned by capture, and no sooner did he marry his latest muse and capture her essence in a new ballet than he started looking elsewhere for inspiration. With Tallchief the gap between appearance and reality was especially wide, for she was no evanescent Osage sylph but a hardworking, hardheaded professional who scrubbed her own floors and played poker after hours with the men of the company.

"I don't need a housewife," Balanchine griped to a friend. "I need a nymph who fills the bedroom and floats out."* He found one under his nose.

Long-legged and long-necked to the point of gawkiness, with delicately chiseled features and a gamine smile, Tanaquil Le Clercq, known to all as "Tanny," was a Balanchine ballet come to life. "Like a lean Giacometti, she reflected modern art," wrote Allegra Kent, who danced with her in Balanchine's *Divertimento No. 15*. Born in 1929, she was the first great dancer to have studied exclusively at the School of American Ballet, and by the time she made her professional debut in *The Four Temperaments* she was fully formed. Tallchief enviously described her as "a coltish creature who still had to grow into her long, spindly legs. Those legs went on forever—it seemed as if her body could barely sustain them. She had the long, willowy look of a fashion model, dressed stylishly in long skirts and sweaters, and had a lovely presence. . . . Tanny didn't have a formal education, yet she was articulate, witty, and chic." A few of her performances were filmed, and in them

---

*What happened there interested him less—at least in Tallchief's case. "Passion and romance didn't play a big role in our married life," she wrote in her autobiography. "We saved our emotion for the classroom. And despite his reputation as a much-married man obsessed with ballerinas, George was no Don Juan. . . . George saved all his energy for work. He made sure we slept in twin beds, perhaps to conserve his energy."

one can see "the scissor legs, the vehement energy, the regal spine, the expansive upper body, the wit, the chic, the joy in movement" to which her friend Holly Brubach paid tribute after Le Clercq's death in 2000. Jerome Robbins fell in love with her at first sight, and for a while they were inseparable. Balanchine teamed them to memorably comic effect in *Bourrée Fantasque*, while Robbins began making dances of his own for her. "All the ballets I ever did for the company," he later confessed, "it was always for Tanny."

But Balanchine's eye had already started to wander—as had Tallchief's. "I have never left any of my wives," he liked to say. "They have all left me." By then he was more than ready for Tallchief to go. "She was like tiger," he told a dancer years later, "and after awhile you get restless and tense living with tiger all the time. Then I found Tanny—she was like flower." Tallchief left him for another man after the London season, and no sooner did NYCB return to Manhattan than he began seeing Le Clercq in public. "I just love you to talk to, to go around with, play games, laugh like hell, etc.," she told Robbins in a letter. "However, I'm in love with George. Maybe it's a case of he got here first." Devastated by what he saw as her betrayal, he made *The Cage*, a chilling portrait of a tribe of insect-women who kill the men with whom they mate. And though Tallchief remained the prima ballerina for a few years more, it was Le Clercq for whom Balanchine made *La Valse* (1951, music by Ravel), a darkly glamorous vignette about a beautiful young girl who encounters a black-clad man at a party. He offers her a pair of black gloves into which she heedlessly plunges her hands. Then they waltz together with wild abandon until she collapses and dies.

La Valse ranks among Balanchine's most striking creations, one with which Le Clercq would forever after be identified, though it was a bizarre present to have offered his latest muse, whom he married at the end of 1952: a ballet in which he envisioned her premature death. What happened to her in real life would be immeasurably more shocking.

WITH BALANCHINE at the helm, Tallchief and Le Clercq onstage, and Robbins contributing to the repertory, it seemed as if Lincoln Kirstein had made good on his rash promise. New York City Ballet was now at least the equal of Ballet Theatre, and many connoisseurs thought it superior. But their opinion was not yet shared by ordinary balletgoers who, like the London critics, found Balanchine's neoclassicism unpleasingly austere. For most Americans, ballet still meant gaudy spectacles danced by exotic butterflies with Russian-sounding names, and while Ballet Theatre obligingly supplied that commodity, City Ballet did not. At the urging of Kirstein and Baum, Balanchine tried out one novelty after another in an attempt to broaden NYCB's appeal. Frederick Ashton made two story ballets, *Illuminations* in 1950 and *Picnic at Tintagel* in 1952; Antony Tudor, on the outs with Ballet Theatre, came aboard as a guest choreographer in 1951, bringing with him Hugh Laing, his lover, and Diana Adams, Laing's wife. (Their uneasy ménage à trois suggested nothing so much as the plot of a Tudor ballet.) Nora Kaye, Tudor's most celebrated interpreter, defected from Ballet Theatre the same year, immediately attracting attention when Robbins cast her in *The Cage*.

Some of these innovations were sound, others misguided, but their overall effect was to dilute the company's still-inchoate style, and Balanchine knew it. Thrown off his creative stride—he had made no ballets of substance since *Orpheus* in 1948—he expressed his concern in a letter to Kirstein: "Until now, somehow we have created new ideas and we were progressive and now the company is established and can perform as well as the other famous companies. But that is not enough. If we continue in the same way we will become standardized, just like the others. We shouldn't do millions of little hors d'oeuvres. It is no longer progressive." What NYCB needed, he knew, was a hit that would attract new audiences, but one consistent with his "progressive" theatrical values. *Firebird* was only a one-act ballet whose appeal had more to do with

Chagall's borrowed decor and Tallchief's dancing than Balanchine's choreography; Kirstein and Baum suggested a new full-evening ballet, something Balanchine had never before attempted, and he chose *The Nutcracker.* Tchaikovsky's score had been popularized by its use in Walt Disney's *Fantasia,* but the ballet itself, originally choreographed by Lev Ivanov in 1892, had rarely been seen onstage in New York. Now Balanchine put together a *Nutcracker* whose first act was a loving evocation of the Christmas celebrations of his St. Petersburg boyhood, followed by a second-act divertissement starring Tallchief as the Sugar Plum Fairy and Le Clercq as Dewdrop, a Balanchine-invented character who leads the Waltz of the Flowers (plus a hoop dance identical to the one with which Balanchine had wowed the crowds at the Maryinsky half a lifetime ago). The students of the School of American Ballet were pressed into service for the Christmas party, and Robbins contributed a fairy-tale skirmish between the Nutcracker and the Mouse King.

Balanchine solved the problem of putting together a child-friendly extravaganza so methodically that those who knew him only casually might well have mistaken his coolheadedness for cynicism. "Everybody always asks why do I want to do *Nutcracker*—even in Russia they ask me," he said. "It's not that I *want* to. It's my business to make repertoire. My approach to the theater—to ballet—is to entertain the public. . . . *Nut-cracker Suite* in America is a free title, a million-dollar title—free. So Baum asked me to do it. I said, 'If I do anything, it will be full-length and very expensive.'" He knew that his *Nutcracker* would have to astonish in order to succeed, and Baum grew nervous as the bills piled up. The biggest single expense was the magic Christmas tree that grows to enormous size midway through the first act. City Center's stage had no trap-doors, meaning that Balanchine and Jean Rosenthal, the lighting designer who did so much to shape the on-stage look of New York City Ballet in its early years, would have to devise and construct a collapsible tree from scratch. Balanchine loved to tell how he tricked Baum into spending more on the tree than he had bud-geted: "Baum gave me $40,000 [for the entire produc-tion]. We studied how the tree could grow both up and also out, like an umbrella. The tree cost $25,000, and as soon as he had to sign the check, Baum was angry. He told Betty [Cage], 'Stop that fool. George, can't you just do it without the tree?' I said, '[The ballet] *is* the tree.' It cost $80,000 instead of $40,000."

"Everyone thought it was a foolhardy, extravagant enterprise that would put us in the poorhouse," Tallchief recalled with amusement—everyone, that is, but Bal-anchine, who knew that the combination of beautiful music, poignant choreography, and a very expensive tree would prove irresistible. The word soon got around that City Ballet had something remarkable on tap, and *Time,* that infallible barometer of middlebrow taste, put Balanchine on its cover the week before opening night, making sure to mention that *The Nutcracker* would include "a Christmas tree as big as Balanchine can fit onto the stage." The premiere took place on February 2, 1954, two weeks after his fiftieth birthday, and it was a smash hit, the biggest and most enduring popular success that New York City Ballet would ever know. Not only did audiences flock to see the magic tree, but most of the critics recognized that Balanchine's *Nutcracker* was not just a crowd-charming confection but an evocation of childhood whose nostalgic sentiments (in Edwin Denby's words) "appear onstage without vulgarization or coyness, with brilliant dancing, light fun, and with the amplitude of a child's wonderful premonitions." Since then, NYCB has performed it every year without fail. CBS telecast the complete ballet in 1957 and 1958, the second time with Balanchine himself playing the cameo role of Herr Drosselmeyer, and not long after that, other dance companies across America started presenting their own *Nutcracker*s. What started out as a calculated bid to put New York City Ballet on a more stable financial and artistic footing mushroomed into a nationwide Christmas tradition.

Seven months later Balanchine pulled yet another rabbit out of his capacious hat, a plotless ballet called *Western Symphony* in which NYCB's dancers dressed up in his favorite cowboy garb and frolicked to Hershy Kay's orchestral variations on such familiar ditties as "Red River Valley" and "Oh, Dem Golden Slippers," with Tanaquil Le Clercq donning a fantastically elaborate hat to sail through a saucy duet with Jacques d'Amboise. Baum capitalized on its success by putting together a "ham-and-eggs" program of four ballets guaranteed to sell out City Center: Balanchine's one-act version of *Swan Lake*, Robbins's *Afternoon of a Faun*, *Firebird*, and *Western Symphony*. Between *Nutcracker* and the ham-and-eggs bill, NYCB had found a way to coin money without compromising its artistic values, and though it would be many more years before the company was financially secure, the days of constant worry were over. Now Balanchine could concentrate on refining the company's style and adding "progressive" dances to its repertory. Little by little, the hors d'oeuvres he had complained about to Kirstein were disappearing from the programs, to be replaced with more substantial fare. A week after *Western Symphony* came the premiere of *Ivesiana*, a joltingly modern tribute to the then-obscure music of Charles Ives. ("Strange music," Le Clercq warned B. H. Haggin, "so the steps are sure to be queerish.") In 1956 Balanchine created *Diverti-mento No. 15,* a Mozart ballet with five starring roles custom-made for Le Clercq, Diana Adams, Melissa Hayden, Allegra Kent, and Patricia Wilde. No other company in America, perhaps none in the world, could have fielded so gifted and varied a group of ballerinas. It seemed as if nothing was beyond Balanchine's reach.

That August the dancers packed their bags and left for a ten-week tour of continental Europe. The performances went well, though there were tensions not far below the surface—it was rumored that Balanchine was pursuing a new love and that he and Le Clercq would soon separate. Then, after a show in Copenhagen, Le Clercq fell ill. "She had just danced the last movement of *Western Symphony,*" remembered Leon Barzin, the company's music director. "I came up and put my scarf around her, she was so wringing wet. The next morning she couldn't get up." The Danish doctors diagnosed polio and put her in an iron lung. Days went by before it was clear that she would survive—barely. At twenty-seven, she was paralyzed from the waist down and would spend the rest of her days in a wheelchair. Once she understood that her dancing career was over, she thought of killing herself. Though she bowed to the inevitable and went on to lead an active and productive life, she would never write her memoirs or talk to reporters or researchers about her life with Balanchine. That was a closed book. Not long before she died, I saw her sitting on the promenade of the New York State Theater, mere paces away from a photo on the wall that showed her dancing gaily with Jerome Robbins in *Bourrée Fantasque*. With her white hair and pale, wrinkled skin, she looked like a chic ghost.

Her fellow dancers were stunned by the news. "That gave me nightmares," Melissa Hayden remembered. "I would dream that she was on stage and that I was excited about her dancing and was congratulating her. She had been so special. It was a tremendous loss to the company, to the shape of the company." Frank O'Hara wrote an "Ode to Tanaquil Le Clercq" in which he called her "perfection's broken heart." As for Balanchine, he was sure he had somehow caused her illness. "I'm sure [he] felt kind of responsible for this happening to Tanny," said one NYCB dancer. "They had already split up. She was driving herself very hard to prove to him, to her mother, to whoever was expecting something of her. She was pushing herself very hard, and she was very run down when she contracted polio."

Beyond that, the superstitious Balanchine felt guilty for less rational reasons. In *La Valse* he had made her the helpless victim of a specter in black; before that, he had choreographed a dance for a March of Dimes benefit in which he cast the fifteen-year-old Le Clercq as a dancer who contracted polio from yet another man in black, this one played by Balanchine himself. Now she had been struck down for real, and he stubbornly blamed himself. He withdrew from New York City Ballet for a full year to take care of her, while Robbins, no less inconsolable, quit the company altogether, not to return until 1969. All their triumphs were as ashes.

Too definite for words: Suzanne Farrell and Peter Martins in the pas de deux of *Concerto Barocco*. Though plotless, *Barocco* exemplifies one of George Balanchine's favorite sayings: "Put a man and a girl on a stage and there is already a story." © *Martha Swope*

Masters of the universe: Serge Diaghilev, the all-powerful Capone of the Ballets Russes, and Igor Stravinsky, his world-famous resident composer, in 1921. Between them, they took a promising young choreographer from Russia and made him immortal. *Hulton Archives/Getty Images*

In the beginning: Serge Lifar and the three muses of *Apollo* (with Alexandra Danilova, left, as Terpsichore). A rare photograph from the original 1928 Ballets Russes production, elaborately designed in the Diaghilev manner by André Bauchant. *Courtesy of: New York City Ballet Archives Ballet Society Collection*

"You want to see things pure and clear." Jacques d'Amboise and the three muses of *Apollo* (from left: Diana Adams, Patricia Wilde, and Jillana). Note the streamlined "black-and-white" practice clothes in which New York City Ballet danced *Apollo* starting in 1957. *Photograph by Fred Fehl, courtesy of: New York City Ballet Archives*

"People have trouble figuring out who I am." Lincoln Kirstein, *eminence grisé* of New York City Ballet, at a rehearsal with Balanchine. Some thought Kirstein crazy, others merely eccentric, but without his unswerving support, Balanchine might never have come to America or emerged as the dominant figure in twentieth-century ballet.   © *Martha Swope*

Into the light: the final tableau of *Serenade*, Balanchine's first American ballet (shown here in a later NYCB performance). Of all the many images of love and loss with which his work is filled, this is the most poignant.   © *Paul Kolnik, courtesy of: New York City Ballet Archives*

Apotheosis: the climax of *The Four Temperaments*. To Jerome Robbins, it suggested "some momentous departure–like interplanetary travelers taking their leave of the world."

In love with death: *La Valse*, 1951, posed in the studio by George
Platt Lynes. Tanaquil Le Clercq, innocent and heedless, prepares to
waltz to her doom with a stranger (Francisco Moncion), having just
put on the black gloves brought by his servant (Edward Bigelow).
Five years later, Balanchine's witty, chic fourth wife was struck down
by polio and never danced again.   *Photograph by George Platt Lynes*

Muse and colleague: Maria Tallchief, Balanchine's third wife,
seduces Robbins, NYCB's number-two man, in *Prodigal Son*, made
for the Ballets Russes in 1929 and revived for Robbins in 1950.
(The costumes were designed by Georges Rouault for the original
production.) Robbins' long relationship with his older mentor was
complex—and competitive.   *Courtesy of: New York City Ballet Archives*

Bodies and souls: Violette Verdy waltzes flirtatiously with Conrad Ludlow and Nicholas Magallanes in *Liebeslieder Walzer*, the most romantic of Balanchine's plotless ballets. (Verdy's frivolity will soon give way to a darker encounter with Magallanes.)   © *Martha Swope*

A king, not a consort: Edward Villella, NYCB's nonpareil male virtuoso, repeals the law of gravity as Oberon in *A Midsummer Night's Dream*, the greatest of Balanchine's story ballets. *Photograph by Fred Fehl*

Don Quixote, 1965: Balanchine as the Don and Suzanne Farrell as his adored Dulcinea. Four years later, his uncontrollable obsession with Farrell would force her out of New York City Ballet—and change the course of his creative life.   *Photograph by Fred Fehl*

Life after Farrell: Peter Martins and Kay Mazzo in the second pas de deux of Balanchine's *Stravinsky Violin Concerto*, the supreme masterpiece of New York City Ballet's Stravinsky Festival.
Photograph by Fred Fehl, courtesy of: New York City Ballet Archives Ballet Society Collection

Sunset: Balanchine rehearsing Mikhail Baryshnikov in *Orpheus*, 1980. (The lyre held by Baryshnikov was designed by Isamu Noguchi for the 1948 premiere.)   *Photo by Costas*

5 • A MORBID INTEREST IN WOMEN

....

*N*O ONE KNOWS exactly what happened between George Balanchine and Tanaquil Le Clercq in the weeks and months before her illness, though it isn't hard to imagine. They had been together since 1950, and she must have wondered whether—or when—he would become fixated on another young dancer. "It was as if he were building these perfect female statues, and the minute they were done he would find another one," said John Clifford, who knew Balanchine in the sixties and seventies. "It sounds cruel, but in a way don't all artists do that? At the time Mr. B was in love with each woman. But there was always, I felt, a reserve there that indicated he knew he was going to be on to the next."

Whatever his intentions may have been, they were changed utterly when he saw Tanny in an iron lung, clinging to life. For the next few months, he left her side as little as possible. He accompanied her to the polio rehabilitation center in Warm Springs, Georgia, and took part in her physical therapy, then moved her to a new apartment in Manhattan that he decorated in a wildly varied hodgepodge of styles in order to divert her. Instead of making new ballets, he fed and nursed her, told her jokes, and promised her she would recover (and apparently believed it, too, at least for a while). He did the shopping and cooking and ironed his own laundry (that, he always said, was when he got his best ideas). At night they had friends over or watched television—everything from *Gunsmoke* to Fred Astaire's made-for-TV specials.* He was as devoted as he had it in him to be, and perhaps even a little more.

Their tragic idyll had to end sooner or later, though no one save for Balanchine himself could have foreseen

---

*Balanchine's lifelong liking for Westerns, which puzzled so many of his acquaintances, was no affectation but a genuine expression of his classicism. "Westerns are the only films that I liked before and still like now," he told Solomon Volkov late in life. "Maybe because there is nothing superfluous in them. Simple things without pretensions—they don't age as quickly. You watch a Western and think, ah! there's *something* to this. . . ."

what was to follow it. Starting in November of 1957, over the course of eight weeks, New York City Ballet premiered four new dances by Balanchine, all of them plotless but otherwise as varied in tone and style as the decor in his apartment. *Square Dance* was a romp to the music of Corelli and Vivaldi, loosely based on square-dance steps and featuring an authentic caller who "led" the cast through Balanchine's elaborate combinations ("Now keep your eyes on Pat / Now see what she is at / Her feet go wickety-wack"). *Stars and Stripes,* Balanchine's Sousa ballet, was a parade-ground festival whose pas de deux, he claimed, was a valentine to Dwight and Mamie Eisenhower. *Gounod Symphony* was a sweet-tempered tribute to French ballet. And—above all—there was *Agon,* a new collaboration with Igor Stravinsky in which Balanchine, building on the still-potent innovations of *The Four Temperaments,* showed the world that a neoclassical ballet could look as contemporary as a mobile by Alexander Calder.

For years Balanchine and Kirstein had been discreetly pestering Stravinsky to give them another Greek-themed score to go with *Apollo* and *Orpheus,* but none of their suggestions interested him. What he wanted to compose for Balanchine, he told his publisher, was "a kind of symphony to be danced." Then, in 1953, Kirstein sent him a copy of François de Lauze's

Apologie de la danse, a treatise on French court dances published in 1623, together with a cover letter outlining Balanchine's latest notion:

> He suggested a competition before the gods; the audience are statues; the gods are tired and old; the dances reanimate them by a series of historic dances, the correct tempi of which you can quite ignore, but they are called courante, bransle, passepied, rigaudon, menuet, etc. etc. It is as if time called the tune, and the dances which began quite simply in the sixteenth century took fire in the twentieth and exploded.

The idea of a competition that made use of Renaissance dance forms hit the target, and Stravinsky, who had been reading T. S. Eliot's "Sweeney Agonistes" with an eye toward adapting it as a ballet, suggested the word *agon,* Greek for "contest," as a title. He started sketching musical ideas and hammering out a scenario in collaboration with Balanchine, who proposed an ensemble of twelve dancers. Stravinsky in turn recommended that it consist of four men and eight women, making many other choreographic suggestions as well. Stravinsky interrupted work on *Agon* to accept a more lucrative commission, while Balanchine was thrown off his stride by Le Clercq's illness, but by the spring of 1957 the score was finished, and Balanchine agreed to come to Los Angeles that June to hear the first concert performance and finalize his plans for the ballet version. It was just. what he needed to rouse himself from his guilt-ridden torpor. "I have been thinking of you all week—George has talked of little else," Le Clercq wrote to Stravinsky and his wife, Vera, from Warm Springs. "He is so excited about seeing you both. I wish I could come and see you, and hear your music, but . . ."

Balanchine returned to the studio as soon as he got back from Los Angeles. "He was like a dynamo," remembered Patricia Wilde, who was featured in *Square Dance*. "It was as though he had been storing up all the things he wanted to do, and he had all these things he wanted to do for us all, and fantastic works were bubbling up inside." Never had he been presented with so challenging a score. "I must try to find some visual equivalent which is a complement; not an illustration," he wrote in a program note for the premiere. "Such music as Stravinsky's cannot be illustrated. *Agon* was invented for dancing, but it is hard to invent dances of a comparable density, quality, metrical insistence, variety, formal mastery or symmetrical asymmetry. . . . [T]his ballet is not a chest of drawers. It is closer to an IBM electronic computer." But Stravinsky's tightly knit music, with its off-center rhythms, vinegar-sharp harmonies, and splintery, percussive timbres, acted on him like a shot of ice-cold vodka, and he rose effortlessly to the occasion.

Premiered on December 1, a week after *Square Dance*, *Agon* was a sensation, the highbrow counterpart of *The Nutcracker* and the first of Balanchine's "black-and-white ballets," the long series of works he would set to twentieth-century music and present in practice clothes on a bare stage.* Its brusque opening caught the audience by the throat:

> The curtain rises on a stage bare and silent. Upstage four boys are seen with their backs to the public and motionless. They wear the company's dance uniform. Lightly they stand in an intent stillness. They whirl, four at once, to face you. The soundless whirl is a downbeat that starts the action. On the upbeat, a fanfare begins, like cars honking a block away.... Meanwhile the boys' steps have been exploding like pistol shots. The steps seem to come in tough, brief bursts.... The energy of it is like that of fifty dancers.

As always, Edwin Denby's description captures the hard-edged mood of *Agon* exactly. It was, as Kirstein

---

Barocco and *The Four Temperaments* had become black-and-white ballets *de facto* when Balanchine scrapped their decor in 1951, but they were conceived as fully decorated Diaghilev-style productions.

had predicted in 1953, an explosion of modern energy ignited with a classical economy of means. This time, though, Denby wasn't alone in his excitement. All the critics were bowled over, in particular by the pas de deux in which Arthur Mitchell twisted the infinitely elastic Diana Adams (who had stayed behind to dance for Balanchine after Tudor and Laing left the company) into improbable shapes whose sexual implications were impossible to ignore. The fact that Mitchell was black added extra excitement to their symbolic coupling, something of which Balanchine was fully aware, though he never went out of his way to underline it. He didn't have to. It was 1957, and black men and white women simply didn't touch one another that way in public—except on the stage of City Center.

"Wonderful! Wonderful!" Stravinsky shouted when he saw *Agon* in the studio for the first time. Balanchine agreed. "In my opinion," he wrote a decade later, "it is his—it is *our*—most perfect work, representing a total collaboration between musician and choreographer."

THE FLOOD OF premieres that followed Balanchine's return to New York City Ballet was no fluke but the beginning of his most sustained period of creativity. Between 1957 and 1969 he made a dozen major ballets and revived *The Seven Deadly Sins* and *La Sonnambula* for Allegra Kent. In 1959 he collaborated with Martha

Graham on *Episodes,* in which New York City Ballet and the Graham company danced to the complete orchestral music of Anton Webern. Graham contributed a dance about Mary, Queen of Scots, Balanchine a plotless, slyly gnomic black-and-white ballet—proof that his neoclassical brand of ballet was at least as up-to-date as Graham's expressionistic brand of modern dance. "It was like watching light pass through a prism," Graham said after watching him at work. "The music passes through him, and in the same natural yet marvelous way that a prism refracts light, he refracts music into dance."*

Paul Taylor, then with the Graham company, danced a solo in Balanchine's portion of *Episodes,* and his autobiography contains an unforgettable portrait of the choreographer:

> He arrives on the dot and shakes my hand while bowing half-humorously. I'm bowing back and, taking him in from his feet upwards, see that he's wearing smart shoes, freshly creased slacks, cow-

---

*Their working methods differed in another way: Balanchine habitually choreographed out of sequence, starting with the musical climaxes and working backward. "I do the finale first," he explained. "Then I know where I'm going, where's the end. You have to know where you're going. If you start on the road, and you don't know where you're going, you never arrive anywhere. So I usually like to finish first, and then I know where my possibilities will be."

boy shirt, and one of his famous string ties. His handshake is run-of-the-mill, and his medium-sized body, though aged, is trim, but it seems never to have been particularly physical. When I get to the eyes, in color and depth of experience they twinkle back darkly. His manner is dry and businesslike yet easy and agreeable. It's plain that if given the chance, most any dancer would happily break his neck in hopes to please him. . . . The speed and craft with which he works are astounding, the rehearsal time being used economically, none of it taken up by explanations of concepts, poetic imagery, or motivation. . . . At the end of the last rehearsal, since the solo seems to be about something, yet its subject a mystery to me, I ask Mr. B if there is any particular way that it's to be danced. "Umm," he answers, nose fidgeting and sniffing out a proper image. "Is like fly in glass of milk, yes?" The picture was perfect.*

---

*For all his reluctance to discuss the specific meanings of his dances, Balanchine often used such poetic metaphors in the studio. He told Edward Villella that the opening of Apollo's solo variation was "like an eagle on a perch, on a rock, looking down from a crag," and he explained to John Clifford that the adagio of *Symphony in C* was a "dance of the moon . . . the *grand jetés* where she gets carried back and forth at one point are supposed to be the moon going across the sky."

The company that once had been known mainly to a coterie of balletomanes, artists, and intellectuals now started turning up in popular magazines like *Life* and on TV programs like the *Ed Sullivan Show*. Never before had ballet been so central to the American cultural conversation—and it happened on George Balanchine's demanding terms. The world had caught up with him at last. Even his native land rediscovered its long-lost son: New York City Ballet toured the Soviet Union in 1962, the first time Balanchine had been there since his defection thirty-eight years before. "Welcome to Russia, home of the classical ballet," a Soviet official told him as he stepped off the plane in Moscow. "Thank you," he replied without missing a beat, "but America is now home of the classical ballet. Russia is home of the old romantic ballet." But that didn't mean he had turned his back on the romanticism of his youth. *Liebeslieder Walzer* (1960, music by Brahms) and *A Midsummer Night's Dream* (1962, music by Mendelssohn), for example, were both profoundly romantic in every sense of the word—as well as formally innovative.

Liebeslieder Walzer was made at the urging of Morton Baum, who liked its plaintive score. It is set not in a sky-blue void but a candle-lit ballroom where four aristocratic-looking young couples in evening dress spend an hour waltzing together, accompanied by the four singers and two pianists with whom they share the stage. The couples are entangled in subtly differing ways (one of the women, for example, appears to be older than her partner-lover), though there is no plot or Tudor-style "acting" to give away their intimate secrets.* Romantic ends are achieved by modern means: all you see are the setting and the steps, with everything else left to the imagination. The dancers drift outdoors into a moonlit garden and the curtain falls for a breathless moment. When it rises again, the ballroom itself is flooded with moonlight, the women are wearing tutus and toe shoes, and the decorous ballroom dancing of the first act is replaced by the heightened gestures of ballet. At the end, the women reappear in their party gowns, and the couples listen in stillness to the last waltz, whose words, sung in German, are by Goethe:

> *Now, Muses, enough!*
> *You strive in vain to show*

---

*Balanchine loathed dancers who emoted onstage like heart-on-sleeve prima donnas, italicizing the feelings he preferred to leave implicit. "That was very good acting—what happened to the dancing?" he would ask. Instead he sought from his dancers a direct, egoless presentation of the emotions with which his dances were filled. ("Don't act with your soul—act with your *role*" was another of his favorite sayings.) Those unable to comply found him implacable. "Don't act," he told Merrill Ashley at a rehearsal of *Swan Lake*. "No acting at all. Don't look at your partner. Don't do anything. Don't pay any attention to him. You just stand there with him to the end of the ballet. In the old days people never got close. You must just stand there." To Edward Villella he was blunter: "Dear, don't be movie actor."

How joy and sorrow alternate in loving hearts.
You cannot heal the wounds inflicted by love;
But assuagement comes from you alone.

"The words ought to be listened to in silence," Balanchine wrote, surely thinking of the joys and sorrows of his own complicated life.

The costume change midway through *Liebeslieder Walzer* is a stroke of fantasy as stunning in its quieter way as the climactic flying lifts of *The Four Temperaments.* Balanchine revealed its meaning to Bernard Taper: "In the first act, it's the real people that are dancing. In the second act, it's their souls." But more than a few members of the ballet's earliest audiences, bored by its unending succession of "love-song waltzes," would slip out of the theater during the pause between acts. In an oft-told anecdote that may or may not be true, Balanchine and Kirstein were watching a performance together. "Look how many people are leaving, George," Kirstein moaned, to which Balanchine replied, "Ah, but look how many are staying!" Today, though New York City Ballet now performs *Liebeslieder Walzer* only infrequently, it is loved by connoisseurs for what Arlene Croce has called its "persistent note of melancholy and tragic remorse," and there are those, myself included, who regard it as their favorite Balanchine ballet of all.

Two years later Balanchine followed it with his first original full-evening story ballet, a dance version of Shakespeare's *Midsummer Night's Dream* in which the plot is propelled, and the characters defined, through fleet-footed movement rather than static mime. Painstakingly augmenting Mendelssohn's familiar incidental music to the play with four less well-known concert overtures and two movements of a string symphony, Balanchine put together a handsomely proportioned two-act score (even the key relations of the various sections are precisely worked out) in which each scene is built around an extended, carefully organized dance sequence rather than a series of short variations, an innovation responsible for the ballet's tremendous forward momentum. The story of the mismatched lovers and the feuding fairies who reunite them is told with witty economy in the first act, followed after intermission by a wedding scene in which the play within a play performed by Bottom and his "rude mechanicals" is replaced by a two-movement divertissement whose pas de deux is one of Balanchine's most tender inspirations.

Le Clercq's illness had forced him to concentrate on the other women of New York City Ballet. He favored Diana Adams, who danced Titania and the "older woman" in *Liebeslieder* (though she was forced to withdraw from the premiere of *A Midsummer Night's*

Dream when she became pregnant by her second husband and subsequently miscarried), but he also made good use of the charm and musicality of Violette Verdy, who danced the *Midsummer* divertissement and the central role in *Liebeslieder,* and of the firm attack of Melissa Hayden, the all-American virtuoso who was taking over Maria Tallchief's parts. None of the men in the company received nearly as much attention. While roles such as Apollo, the Prodigal Son, and the two male variations in *The Four Temperaments* were very much a part of his ballets, his interest in women as dancers had long been far more pronounced. "Ballet is woman," he liked to say. "Man is an attendant to a queen. He is consort, he is noble, brilliant, but finally merely good enough to be her partner." To William Weslow he put it more crudely: "Man must be subservient. Is nothing. Is rotten. Woman is everything. Puts foot up. Shits on him. Pisses on him." No other remark offers a more revealing glimpse into the peculiarities of his psyche. Still, Balanchine's gynocentric vision of ballet was more than merely pathological: it was a conviction arising from a lifetime's observation. He believed that women's bodies were perfect instruments for ballet, combining the best features of cats and horses. "Women are more flexible," he insisted. "They have more ideal body for ballet for technique, for speed, for fine technique. Boys made to jump, to lift the girl, support the girl. But boys don't have speedy legs because they are not built that way."

Such was his choreographic credo, but he never let theory interfere with practice, and in Edward Villella he had a male dancer good enough to be not just a consort but a king. The women of New York City Ballet had always been more impressive than the men, though Jacques d'Amboise, who became a principal dancer in 1953, had the technical facility lacking in the otherwise excellent dancing of Nicholas Magallanes (the first Orpheus) and Francisco Moncion, the company's other two leading men. So did Villella, a high-flying, forthrightly masculine virtuoso who inspired Balanchine (and thrilled the public) as had no other male dancer. In 1960 Balanchine replaced Moncion with Villella in *Prodigal Son;* two years later he made him Oberon, King of the Fairies, in *A Midsummer Night's Dream,* creating for him one of the most technically challenging variations ever made for a man. "I remember one of his exits that used to hit the audience like a joke—a high jeté-flip in which he reversed his pose and soared backwards into the wings," Arlene Croce wrote after his retirement. "In another passage, he flew backwards at top speed, sitting on air and kicking air away like a tiresome footstool."

Even more memorable is the first-act pas de deux that Titania dances with Bottom after Puck has turned him into a donkey at Oberon's urging. Bottom plays the scene for laughs, but his new lover shines with sincerity, and the contrast between their conditions is at once preposterous and poetic. Once again, the autobiographical overtones are impossible to ignore: Balanchine never thought himself physically attractive, and he must have had that in mind when he envisioned a man in a donkey's head partnering the beautiful Diana Adams.* By then, of course, he had long since succumbed to the lifelong compulsion he had suppressed for as long as he could. According to Lucia Davidova, his friend and confidante, "He became desperate about Diana Adams. He was really in love with her, but his wife was an invalid and he didn't know what to do about it. He tried for three years or so. Then finally he said to his wife, as he told me, 'Tanny, if I go on with my marriage, I think I'll stop creating. I know the stimulus. In order to continue working I have to follow my love.'" The cycle of pursuit and disillusion had begun once more.

Well into middle age Balanchine hungered, in Allegra Kent's tart phrase, to add more Lolitas to his bal-

---

*According to *Time*'s 1954 cover story, "Balanchine was a good dancer, but his build was slight for a top *danseur noble*. Moreover, says Balanchine now, pushing up his nose with a forefinger and displaying his teeth, 'I looked in the mirror. Some people say it was not true, but I looked like a rat.'"

lerina gallery. To another dancer he confessed that he even enjoyed the smell of women: "When they get heated up, to put nose in certain places when they do exercise . . . odor wafts out and it's natural, it's natural. This I like." Kent, with whom he was briefly (and productively) infatuated, noticed that his major romances all lasted for roughly seven years apiece, and that he usually married the women in question when they were twenty-one years old. Only one thing had changed: they were as young as ever, but he was growing older, and the days when he could take for granted the unquestioning devotion of any woman in the company were running short. Kent, for one, kept him at arm's length, and when Adams married Ronald Bates, the company's stage manager, he told Davidova, "Somebody just put their hand on my head and is holding me under the water, and I don't know when I'll come up."

"He's the most secure man I've ever met in my life," the famously insecure Lincoln Kirstein had marveled. No more. From his earliest days in the company, Villella noticed that anyone who "detracted from the chosen ballerina" by diverting attention from her onstage was likely to suffer for it. Now Balanchine stopped limiting his smothering embrace to the chosen one. It became his policy to discourage all the women of New York City Ballet from marrying: "For a female dancer, marriage means the end of her individuality. . . . When you marry, you become Mrs. Him." Some took great pains to conceal their romantic involvements from him, though he almost always found out anyway, and his desire to control their private lives grew more pronounced with every passing year, just as he hated for a dancer to perform elsewhere between seasons without his permission, or take class from anyone but him.* He even gave his favorite ballerinas different brands of perfume so that he would know when they were in the theater, and in the studio he sometimes behaved toward them as though he were a feudal lord entitled by divine right to the droit du seigneur. "Balanchine loved *Liebeslieder*," said Melissa Hayden, "and he was in love with his girls in it. He couldn't take his hands off me. When the four couples got together for the finale, he would look at us and caress my neck, and I would look at him and think, 'What's he going to do now? Everybody else is watching.'"

---

*This became a problem for those dancers who, like Villella and Robert Weiss, felt that Stanley Williams, a teacher from the Royal Danish Ballet School whom Balanchine had brought to America to work with the company, was able to articulate the underlying principles of Balanchine's style more effectively than Balanchine himself, who used his company classes less as a means of developing his dancers' bodies than as (in Villella's words) a "lab for his choreographic experiments." As a result, Balanchine banished Williams to the School of American Ballet, where he soon established himself as one of the most influential dance teachers of the postwar era.

Those who rebelled learned that he had a hundred ways of expressing his displeasure: they might be dropped from their favorite roles, or ordered to wear unflattering costumes. Such was life in a company organized to serve the whims of an all-seeing genius. "He oversaw everything that went on in that house: who was there, who wasn't, who was lazy, who was ambitious, who worked and who didn't work, who got paid, how much, who got paid too much, who was underpaid," Richard Tanner said. "He'd check programs to see how the information was printed. He'd change it around if he didn't like it. He worked. He was there all the time." Above all, he was constantly looking for young dancers capable of arousing his imagination, and in 1963 he found a new one, a prodigiously gifted teenager from Ohio whose destiny it was to break his heart.

ROBERTA SUE FICKER was one of Cincinnati's promising young ballet students when Diana Adams saw her on a scouting trip for the School of American Ballet in 1960 and told her to come to New York and audition. She danced for Balanchine on her fifteenth birthday, received a full scholarship, and set about learning the elements of his style; a year later she became a member of New York City Ballet. Finding her triple-barreled name insufficiently romantic for ballet, she dubbed herself "Suzanne Farrell" and plunged into the whirl-wind routine of brand-new members of the NYCB corps, learning new roles on a sink-or-swim basis. Jacques d'Amboise had already noticed her in adagio class, and Balanchine started to pay closer attention to her dancing during the company's tour of the Soviet Union. She soon mastered the bit parts used to try out NYCB's newest members, and all who saw her thought she would become a very good dancer.

In 1963 Balanchine made *Movements for Piano and Orchestra*, an unprecedentedly complex black-and-white ballet for Adams and d'Amboise set to a brist-lingly atonal Stravinsky score. Once again Adams was forced to withdraw at the last minute because of a pregnancy (which ended, like the one before it, in a miscarriage), and Balanchine, furious at what he took to be the betrayal of his former lover, would have can-celed the premiere had d'Amboise not persuaded him to try Farrell out as a replacement. Adams taught her the steps in two intense hours of coaching, the per-formance went on as scheduled, and the critics were wowed. So was Stravinsky, who went out of his way to ask Balanchine about the new dancer. "Igor Fyodor-ovich, this is Suzanne Farrell," the choreographer told him gleefully. "Just been born."

The girl who caught Igor Fyodorovich's eye had a catlike face, a touch of baby fat, and exceptionally long legs (she was over six feet tall on pointe). She also had the same high-stepping energy as Tanaquil Le Clercq, though she was less distinctive looking and not nearly so individual a personality: Le Clercq was stylish and clever, Farrell shy and naive. But she was determined to dance in whatever way would please Balanchine, however extreme, and her pliability excited him. Shortly after the premiere of *Movements*, Balanchine told her that he was going to make a pas de deux for her to dance with d'Amboise. He then left for Germany, where he staged *Orpheus and Eurydice* for the Hamburg State Opera.* From there he sent her a handwritten letter containing a poem scrawled in capital letters:

> *I CAN'T FORGET THIS BLESSED VISION,*
> *IN FRONT OF ME YOU STOOD MY LOVE,*
> *LIKE INSTANT MOMENT OF DECISION,*
> *LIKE SPIRIT BEAUTEOUS FROM ABOVE.*

Balanchine scrupulously explained that the poem was meant to show "how Jacques should feel when he

---

*Balanchine's interest in opera was serious and lifelong, and in addition to his various versions of *Orpheus* and *L'Enfant et les sortilèges*, he also directed Tchaikovsky's *Yevgeny Onegin* and Glinka's *Ruslan and Ludmilla* in Hamburg and staged the American premiere of Stravinsky's *The Rake's Progress* for the Metropolitan Opera in 1953.

is dancing pas de deux with you," but *Meditation,* a sentimental vignette (set, significantly, to the music of Tchaikovsky) in which a man whose hair has started to turn gray dances with his ideal woman, left little doubt in anyone else's mind that Farrell was his own "blessed vision." He promptly began putting her into Adams's other roles, starting with *Liebeslieder Walzer.* "He radiated a warmth and delicacy that was nice to be around," Villella remembered. "The studio—the theater itself— seemed bathed in a glow."

This time, though, the object of his obsession was forty-two years his junior, and for all Farrell's devotion to her new mentor, the difference in their ages ultimately proved too great to bridge. "It's hard to talk to young women when you're not so young, when you're over fifty," Balanchine later said. "If they're seventeen, they want seventeen-year-old friends. Of course, you can be philosophical about it: what is, is, what will be, will be. But it can still annoy you, especially if you don't want to make a nice impression but are seriously attracted." (That it might be inappropriate for a fifty-nine-year-old man to be seriously attracted to a seventeen-year-old girl seems not to have occurred to him.) At the time he expressed his frustration more petulantly to Lucia Davidova: "When he originally met [Farrell] she was not really a companion for him, culturally. . . . He said, 'I introduce her to Stravinsky and

Tchelitchev and other people, yet I'm fully aware that she'd rather chat with her girlfriends from the ballet school about nothing.'" Farrell herself would guilelessly tell a journalist, "I think I was a sort of relief to him. He doesn't expect a girl to be intellectual—and I found I could make him laugh."

In any case, he was attracted not by Farrell's tenuous conversational skills but by her immense potential as a dancer. New York City Ballet was a year away from abandoning the cramped stage and grubby backstage quarters of City Center for the New York State Theater at Lincoln Center, a house of mammoth proportions whose proscenium arch was fifty-one feet high.* Balanchine knew that a larger stage would demand dancing to match. "We were not used to jumping that far, running that far, or being carried that far," Farrell would later write, "and the whole company suddenly

---

*In that same year, New York City Ballet and the School of American Ballet also received a $5 million grant from the Ford Foundation "to strengthen professional ballet in America," the largest single-source donation ever made in support of dance. The grant was hugely controversial—no other company received anything remotely approaching that much money, while American Ballet Theatre got none at all—but it made NYCB financially secure at long last, simultaneously turning Balanchine and Kirstein into the most powerful institutional figures in American dance. (As a condition of the grant, Balanchine was required to accept an annual salary of $10,000, which he secretly used to hire Barbara Horgan as his full-time personal assistant.)

seemed to be out of breath." But Villella was up to the challenge, and Balanchine saw in Farrell a ballerina capable of making the same kind of impact. He constantly urged her to dance bigger and faster, to take more chances, and she obliged. Later on Adams asked him what it was about Farrell's dancing that had captured his imagination, and he replied, "Well, you see, dear, Suzanne never *resisted*."

Soon she was dancing every night, while the other ballerinas found themselves dancing less than they liked. "It was hard to hold your own," said Hayden, who had previously been considered Tallchief's successor as the prima ballerina of City Ballet. "No one else danced. There was no transition—it was as though he had closed a book of his life and picked up another book, turned to the first page, and there was Suzanne. He loved the new crop of dancers, they had beauty, they had 'bigness'—we were going into a new theater, and he wanted 'bigness.'" Even after the company moved to Lincoln Center in 1964, not everyone liked what Farrell was doing with Balanchine's choreography. Some critics found it excessive and exaggerated, but surviving TV broadcasts from the sixties, most notably a phenomenal *Apollo* taped in Canada in 1969, suggest that she was in fact realizing Le Clercq's unfulfilled promise, though her shyness made her seem elusive and mysterious onstage rather than witty and gay. But whatever the critics may have thought, Balanchine was seeing what he wanted to see—both onstage and off. When the dance critic Walter Terry inquired in 1962 about writing his biography, Balanchine had ordered Betty Cage to tell him that "my personal life is not very interesting. . . . If Terry wants to know about my inspiration or who is my Muse then he will never know that. Because I won't tell him." Now he didn't have to: it was all in the programs.

The difference was that Balanchine was no longer a craftsman laboring in obscurity but a world-famous ballet master married to a much-loved woman who looked on from her wheelchair as her lawful wedded husband courted his latest Lolita more and more openly. Robert Garis, a critic who kept close tabs on the company, never forgot the night when Le Clercq "was present at Farrell's first *Swan Lake* . . . when Balanchine came down the staircase from his customary vantage point at the back of the first ring, he went not to Le Clercq, from whom he was long estranged, but backstage to Farrell." Nor did it stop there. He made a full-evening ballet version of *Don Quixote* (1965, music by Nabokov) in which Farrell was cast as Dulcinea, with Balanchine himself playing the Don at the premiere and on several other occasions, dancing a pas de deux in which he pursued her on his knees. It was Titania and Bottom writ large, and though the results were uneven (albeit interestingly so), forcing him to spend years fussing with *Don Quixote* before finally dropping the ballet from the repertory in 1978, it served the purpose of thrusting him and his Dulcinea into the spotlight—and the gossip columns.

Don Quixote put Le Clercq in an impossible position. Balanchine had hitherto carried on his affairs with discretion, but now he was shouting his love for Farrell from the stage of the State Theater. "How could Tanny bear this?" Allegra Kent wrote. "I never was able to look at the ballet again; all I could see in it was gloom and disloyalty." They separated for a time, reconciled, then parted permanently. Meanwhile, Farrell remained the prima ballerina *assoluta* of New York City Ballet. In 1967 Balanchine made *Jewels,* a triptych of one-act dances set to the music of Fauré, Stravinsky, and Tchaikovsky and misleadingly billed as the first full-evening plotless ballet (the dances are in fact unrelated and can also be performed separately). Violette Verdy was elegant in "Emeralds," Villella sportive and impish in "Rubies," but no one failed to notice that the main event of the evening—if by no means the best of the three dances—was "Diamonds," yet another of Balanchine's Tchaikovsky-accompanied evocations of imperial Russia, at the end of which Farrell was all but crowned queen of New York City Ballet.

The company's collective bemusement at Balanchine's romance was turning to anger. "I have a right to love," he told Patricia Neary when she confronted him.

"You should love all eighty of us," she retorted, and quit. What few knew was that Farrell, as she later admitted in her autobiography, was "overwhelmed and perplexed" by the situation in which she now found herself. It was understood, inside and outside NYCB, that Balanchine longed to marry her: he gave her a ring and incautiously told a Chicago columnist that they were engaged. "I was flattered by his attentions, personal and professional," she wrote, "yet I wasn't prepared to face the consequences of where those attentions might lead." He was married, she was Catholic, and in any case she was sure that to sleep with him, with or without benefit of clergy, would be an irreversible mistake:

> Our unique relationship had proved itself so often to both of us, and it might not have withstood consummation. The physical side of love is of paramount importance to many people, but to us it wasn't. Our interaction was physical, but its expression was dance. . . . He had tried many times before to unify his artistic and emotional passions of the moment, but the history of his many marriages suggested only insecurity to me.

Though both were wracked with guilt over his treatment of Le Clercq, Balanchine remained "unrelenting" in his determination to possess Farrell completely: "He was going to have what he wanted. He always had." At one point she considered committing suicide. Then the impasse was broken in a totally unexpected way when she fell in love with Paul Mejia, a young member of the NYCB corps in whom Balanchine had taken a paternal interest. "I wanted peace," she wrote, "and thought that once I married, George would have to let me go." When Balanchine became aware that she and Mejia were seeing one another on their own time (it was reported in the *New York Post*), he sought to force the issue, first by taking Mejia's roles away from him, then by obtaining a Mexican divorce from Le Clercq in 1969, two weeks after his sixty-fifth birthday. Seventeen days later, while Balanchine was staging another opera in Hamburg, Farrell and Mejia were wed at the Church of St. Paul the Apostle, two blocks from the State Theater.

Balanchine came back to New York in April to prepare for the company's spring gala. It was to be a particularly festive event: Jerome Robbins had returned to NYCB after thirteen years to make *Dances at a Gathering,* an hour-long piano-accompanied ballet to the music of Chopin whose first public performance was set for that evening. Edward Villella, cast in Robbins's new dance, asked to be replaced in the bravura third movement of *Symphony in C,* which followed *Dances at a Gathering* on the bill. Though Mejia was Villella's understudy, another dancer was chosen in his place, and he told Farrell that Balanchine's refusal to let him perform left him no choice but to resign. Balanchine was no longer speaking to Farrell ("Mr. B, if he saw me coming down the corner, would turn the other way"), so she sent him a message saying that if Mejia did not dance in *Symphony in C,* they would both quit. "It had the form of an ultimatum, but, incredible as it seems, I had never intended it to be one," she recalled.

Balanchine chose instead to replace *Symphony in C* with *Stars and Stripes,* and Farrell cleaned out her dressing room. Four days later she and Mejia announced their resignations from the company, telling the press what had happened. Balanchine responded by denying everything: "Could anyone really think I would change a whole program just to keep someone from dancing? Paul was being used according to his ability. Fortunately, or unfortunately, I must make the artistic decisions. . . . After this, it would not be good for the company if they returned." He said he was "disappointed" in Farrell, adding, "She is an exceptional dancer, and we will miss her. . . . Many other companies would be delighted to have her." Such was his cold farewell to the woman he had courted so passionately—and publicly—for the past six years. Late one night Farrell and her new husband went to the State Theater to practice in an empty studio. "You can't come in here," an embarrassed security guard told the equally embarrassed couple.

No American dance company would offer either of them a job, presumably out of fear of antagonizing Balanchine, so they fled to Brussels to dance with Maurice Béjart's Ballet du XXème Siècle, an avant-garde troupe popular in Europe but dismissed by most stateside ballet critics as vulgar and sensationalistic. Meanwhile, Farrell had become an unperson in the theater where she had once reigned as queen. Lincoln Kirstein mentioned her only in passing in *The New York City Ballet* (1973), his official history of the company. Balanchine said nothing at all about her—at least not by name. "Women like you better when you don't hang on them," he told a reporter. "That is how they are. But I am going to tell you this: I am free. I am old man. And nobody is going to get me any more."

6 · LIKE ENTERING HEAVEN

··

*B*ALANCHINE DIDN'T give up women once Suzanne Farrell vanished from his life, but there would be no more self-lacerating obsessions with teenagers. Instead, he began seeing Karin von Aroldingen, a German dancer who had joined New York City Ballet in 1962, not long after Farrell. Born in 1942, Aroldingen was married—she became close to Balanchine during a period of estrangement from her husband—and had a daughter. Their relationship eventually became as much familial as anything else, and it gave him a kind of stability that had been missing from his life, which grew even simpler than before now that he was alone. He still did his own shopping and ironed his own shirts; more and more he kept to himself after hours, watching TV to relax. In time he admitted to others, and perhaps even to himself, that his relentless pursuit of Farrell had been a mistake. "You know, I wasn't meant to marry Suzanne," he told his doctor several years later. "It was God's decision." For now, her parts were divided up among other dancers, most notably the fragile-looking Kay Mazzo, who gracefully took over the lion's share of Farrell's repertory. He had already made major roles for the warmly appealing Patricia McBride, Edward Villella's onstage partner, in *Tarantella* (1964, music by Gottschalk), *Harlequinade* (1965, music by Drigo), and "Rubies," and McBride's importance to the company increased still further as Balanchine began reassembling the pieces of his creative life.

At first it was slow going. *Who Cares?* (1970, music by Gershwin), the first large-scale dance he made after Farrell's departure (and one whose title was generally thought to refer to her), featured Aroldingen, McBride, and Marnee Morris, with smaller solo roles for several other women in the company. A tribute to the great American songwriter with whom he had once hoped to work, *Who Cares?* was popular, but it proved over time to be slighter than was originally thought. The following year saw two flops, *Concerto for Jazz Band and Orchestra* (1971, music by Liebermann), an abortive collaboration with Dance Theatre of Harlem, the all-black classical company Arthur Mitchell had launched after retiring from the stage (and for which Tanaquil Le Clercq was now working as a coach), and *PAMTGG* (1971, music by Kellaway), based on a commercial jingle for an airline, "Pan Am Makes the Going Great," that had briefly tickled Balanchine's fancy. He would premiere no more dances for a full year, warning Kirstein that he was "no longer a cash cow that can be milked for ballets." Meanwhile, Jerome Robbins, who had given up Broadway for ballet, followed up the critical and popular success of *Dances at a Gathering* with a string of ambitious new works that set the critics to buzzing. Was the sixty-seven-year-old Balanchine past his prime? Might the time be ripe for New York City Ballet to consider a change at the top?

Robbins had turned fifty in 1968, but middle age had failed to make him any easier a colleague. If anything, his temperamental behavior in the studio, so different from Balanchine's calm, businesslike demeanor, had grown still more trying. In addition, his work on Broadway had made him rich and famous—he was directing *West Side Story, Gypsy,* and *Fiddler on the Roof* while Balanchine was making ballets without a salary—and he was disinclined to take no for an answer from anyone. As before, Balanchine handled him with kid gloves, inviting Robbins to share his fourth-floor office and never publicly chastising him for the way he treated dancers.* "Mr. B loved [*Dances at a Gathering*], he loved it—and he said, 'You know why I brought Jerry to the company to do this ballet?'" said Patricia McBride. "I said, 'Why?' He said, 'Because Jerry's good. He's good, he's a good choreographer.'. . . Mr. B used to watch every performance from the wings." Violette Verdy agreed:

> Balanchine had a tremendous admiration for Jerry. And very often, probably, had a little tang of thinking that Jerry was more gifted than he was, because the comparison that Balanchine made was at the level of judging himself as only a craftsman. Balanchine never admitted the idea that he might have genius. . . . He thought he was a tremendously good craftsman. And he looked at Jerry, who was not as good a craftsman, yet with wonder and admiration he felt Jerry was even more gifted than him. I could tell that. Isn't that amazing? And he would watch Jerry with tenderness and emotion, like a son who was more gifted than the father.

---

*"Mr. B, I don't know what to do about Jerry," John Clifford complained one day, to which Balanchine replied, "You know, dear, he will teach you how not to treat people."

Yet it wasn't quite that simple. It was true, for instance, that Balanchine watched every performance of *Dances at a Gathering*—but as certain of the dancers came running off the stage, he would hiss to them, "How you like ballet by Jerry the fairy?" He had always been (and would continue to be) scrupulously tolerant of the homosexuals with whom he worked, perhaps because he knew they would never compete with him for the attentions of the women dancers he favored. But just as Balanchine and Robbins had once competed for the love of Tanaquil Le Clercq, so they were now vying for the favor of the public, and Robbins, at least for the moment, was winning.

For his part, Robbins thought Balanchine the master of masters. "When I watch Balanchine work," he wrote in his journal in 1971, "it's so extraordinary I want to give up." His admiration was so great that he spent most of the latter part of his career making plotless ballets, even though not a few of his admirers felt the idiom did not come naturally to so character-driven an artist.* Still, he longed for recognition as a

---

*Robbins himself came to suspect as much. "At NYCB I've fallen backward & [been] put asleep by trying to trust more the GB vocabulary—it's lazy.... [I] know that trying to 'do' a Balanchine-like work is a futile effort—like trying to paint a Leonardo-like painting," he confessed in another journal entry written after Balanchine's death.

master in his own right and complained when critics refused to give it to him. "It was, 'Why was Balanchine always the best?' When would he be the best?" said Penelope Dudleston, one of the few New York City Ballet dancers to whom he became personally close.

THE ANSWER CAME with a vengeance in the spring of 1972. The New York State Theater went dark for a week, then reopened on June 18 for the most ambitious undertaking New York City Ballet had ever attempted, a weeklong Stravinsky Festival at which thirty-one different ballets were performed, twenty of them new, including eight premieres by Balanchine and four by Robbins (plus a new version of *Pulcinella* that the two men choreographed jointly). Balanchine set the tone on opening night by detonating two masterpieces in a row, *Symphony in Three Movements* and *Stravinsky Violin Concerto*. The remainder of the week was a dizzying welter of sight and sound, concluding with an undanced concert performance of Stravinsky's Symphony of Psalms. On the way out of the theater, everyone was handed a shot of vodka to toast the memory of NYCB's patron saint, who had died the preceding April. Richard Buckle, who had flown over from England to cover the proceedings for the London *Sunday Times,* told his readers that "to climb the steps to the golden promenade of the

State Theatre at Lincoln Center for the week of Stravinsky ballets is like entering heaven."

A year and a day before opening night, as Balanchine and Barbara Horgan stood backstage waiting for the curtain to go up on *PAMTGG,* he had turned to her and said, "Next year, Stravinsky." Though his reputation was then at one of its lowest ebbs, he hurled himself into preparations for the festival, informing NYCB's board of directors that it would *have* to open on Stravinsky's ninetieth birthday, and that regardless of cost, the company would *have* to close up shop for a full week of rehearsals. The board capitulated, after which he met with the press to tell them of his plans: "We will show Stravinsky's life through sound and then you will see the whole thing in front of you. . . . He was like Einstein—nobody like him." By that time the rest of the company was hypnotized by his exuberant determination. "George opened a window and said we were going to fly," Robbins said. "We just followed him."

Among those who followed him out the window was Peter Martins, who had come to NYCB from the Royal Danish Ballet in 1969. Martins had initially found the company's style confusing. "The dancers neglected or didn't bother with precision," he recalled. "The emphasis was on the energy and on movement itself, on timing and quickness." Balanchine in turn found Martins's dancing unsatisfactory and started taking roles away from him. When he asked what was wrong, the answer he received was devastating: "You see, dear, you don't seem to be interested. I never see you anywhere, not in class, maybe in O'Neal's restaurant [a dancers' hangout across the street from the State Theater]. When people show interest, I use them. If they don't, I leave them alone. And you don't show interest." Martins swore to do better, and by the time of the festival, Balanchine was ready to take another chance on him, casting the tall, blond-headed *danseur noble* in two new ballets, *Duo Concertant* and *Stravinsky Violin Concerto.* Martins knew it was his last chance to make good, and he threw himself into rehearsals with unprecedented fervor.

As it happened, he had been picked for two of the three major ballets to come out of the Stravinsky Festival (the third, *Symphony in Three Movements,* being a vehicle for Edward Villella). In *Duo Concertant* he danced a pas de quatre with Kay Mazzo and a pair of musicians, a violinist and pianist, who played Stravinsky's score onstage. Martins would also partner Mazzo in Balanchine's second attempt to choreograph the concerto Stravinsky had composed for Samuel Dushkin in 1931. *Balustrade,* the elaborately decorated first version, had vanished after a single performance by the Original Ballet Russe in 1941. Now Balanchine stripped his dancers down to practice clothes and completely restaged the concerto as a black-and-white ballet based on "nothing but pure music." At sixty-eight he had never made a Stravinsky ballet without the advice of the composer, and just as *Stravinsky Violin Concerto* was Martins's last chance to prove himself to Balanchine, it was also Balanchine's first chance to prove himself to everyone else.

The opening toccata is a witty exposition of neo-classical dance logic that takes up where *The Four Temperaments* leaves off. As Stravinsky's bright, dry score ticks away in the background, Balanchine deals his cards faceup: first Mazzo dances with four men, then Karin von Aroldingen dances with four other men, then Jean-Pierre Bonnefous and Martins dance in turn with two different quartets of women. Then the sequence is inverted, the women dancing with women and the men with men—until Martins saunters on alone. The surprise was typical of Balanchine, who made a point of breaking up the symmetrical patterns of classical ballet in order to keep his audiences on their toes. ("Perfect is boring," he liked to say.) The effect is at once bracingly exact and wonderfully good-humored, as if the *Agon* ensemble had been reunited for a series of vaudeville turns.

Next comes a pair of pas de deux, the first a friendly competition in which Aroldingen and Bonnefous leap and strut like a pair of rubber-legged thoroughbreds. In the second, set to a ravishing Bach-like aria "sung" by the violinist, Martins gently steers Mazzo through a maze of poses, sculpting her slender body with the tenderness of a choreographer breaking in a new muse. He stands behind her and they bow together, a gesture that, according to Balanchine, was "as if to say, 'How do you do, Stravinsky?'" Then he curls his outstretched arm and covers her eyes, a gesture, first seen in *Serenade*, which was one of the most emotion-charged motifs in Balanchine's private lexicon of dance metaphor. No sooner do they leave the stage than the rest of the ensemble comes charging back for a lively finale in which Balanchine fills the stage to overflowing with blindingly precise movement. Before long, all twenty dancers are jumping like a gymful of jitterbugs. Then— for the first and only time in the entire dance—the corps pairs off in couples as the music scampers joyously to its final cadence.

Balanchine later told Aroldingen and McBride that *Stravinsky Violin Concerto* was the best ballet he had ever made. To a friend he expressed himself only slightly more modestly: "It is very good! My other ballets? . . . Okay, but not so good." Had the composer lived to see it, he might well have echoed the tribute he paid to *Movements for Piano and Orchestra:* "To see Balanchine's choreography of the *Movements* is to hear the music with one's eyes; and this visual hearing has been a greater revelation to me, I think[,] than to anyone else. The choreography emphasizes relationships of which I had hardly been aware—in the same way—and the performance was like a tour of a building for which I had drawn the plans but never explored the result." Thirty years later the significance of *Stravinsky Violin Concerto* is clearer still, for in no other ballet, not even *Liebeslieder Walzer*, did Balanchine fuse the modern and romantic sides of his personality more indissolubly. It is the ultimate expression of his black-and-white style, and though it may not be his greatest ballet, it is his most perfect one. All those skeptics who had wondered whether the time had come for Balanchine to be put out to pasture wondered no longer: he was still the best. Nobody else came close.

THE STRAVINSKY FESTIVAL, like the miraculous season of *Agon, Square Dance,* and *Stars and Stripes,* marked the beginning of another long period of creative renewal, as well as the renewal of a creative relationship that had been sundered by anger and grief. Early in 1974 Balanchine received a two-sentence letter from Suzanne Farrell: "As wonderful as it is to see your ballets, it is even more wonderful to dance them. Is this impossible?" He responded at once, and a few months later Farrell returned to New York City Ballet. Never again would she be intimate with Balanchine, but he started making dances for her again, and a few years later he even brought himself to admit over dinner that he had acted like a fool:

> I had expected the usual pleasant evening of good wine, food, and conversation but suddenly George started talking about the Bible. I was silent while he recited the Lord's Prayer in Latin and went on to discuss *tentationem*—temptation.... [H]e said, "You know, I was wrong. I was an old man, and you were young. I should not have thought of you that way. You should have had your marriage." Desperately uncomfortable and embarrassed, I kept saying, "No, no, no," but he continued to talk. I felt as if I were listening to a confession I was unworthy to hear.

In an act of public contrition, he featured her in *Chaconne* (1976, music by Gluck), spinning the ballet music from *Orpheus and Eurydice* into a suite of dances prefaced by a quiet, unassuming pas de deux in which Farrell walks with her partner beneath a Balanchine-blue sky full of clouds. After that came *Vienna Waltzes*, his farewell to the protean dance form that had already inspired him to make *La Valse* and *Liebeslieder Walzer*. Premiered in 1977, *Vienna Waltzes* is the most effective of the showy ballets Balanchine called "applause machines," set to the music of Johann Strauss, Franz Lehár, and Richard Strauss and danced on a fantastically elaborate set by Rouben Ter-Arutunian that changes before the audience's eyes from the Vienna Woods to an elegant café, then to a ballroom whose walls are mirrors. Toward the end Farrell drifts out from the wings, waltzing alone—or perhaps with an invisible partner—until she is joined by a male dancer, then by the entire company. It immediately became one of her signature roles, and when she retired from the stage in 1989, it was the last role she danced.

Vienna Waltzes, Farrell wrote, was "perhaps the single most successful ballet in the New York City Ballet's box-office history." It was also the beginning of the end. The following year Balanchine had a heart attack and drew up a will. "Sometime after *Vienna Waltzes*," a member of the company recalled, "it occurred to us he wasn't going to be there forever. He always seemed so young, and then all of a sudden he started to seem older." His condition gradually deteriorated further, forcing him to undergo heart bypass surgery in 1979 and thereby making it impossible for him to take full advantage of the talents of the company's newest member, Mikhail Baryshnikov, who had left American Ballet Theatre at the age of thirty in order to learn from the reigning master of neoclassical ballet. Though Baryshnikov danced in numerous Balanchine ballets during his brief stint with NYCB, including *Apollo, Prodigal Son, Orpheus,* and "Rubies," he never quite got the hang of his new teacher's speeded-up version of classical style.* Still, Balanchine gave him ample encouragement and claimed to like what he was doing. The two became friends—even now, Balanchine continued to be more comfortable with his Russian-speaking acquaintances—and their friendship survived Baryshnikov's decision to depart NYCB after a year and become ABT's artistic director. "I'll never regret that I worked with him," the dancer later said.

Alas, Balanchine made no new roles for Baryshnikov. Indeed, he had only two ballets of importance left in him, *Robert Schumann's "Davidsbündlertänze"* (1980, music by Schumann), a semiautobiographical fantasy reminiscent of *Liebeslieder Walzer,* and *Mozartiana* (1981, music by Tchaikovsky), his final attempt at a score with which he had been preoccupied since the days of Les Ballets 1933, this time transformed into a heartfelt tribute to Farrell's pristinely poetic dancing. Not only had

---

*"He was very much used to taking a long, deep plié," wrote Villella, who worked with Baryshnikov on several of his old roles. "He wasn't accustomed to landing and using the landing as the position from which to attack the next step. Now as he worked, he took his time doing the plié. . . . I confess to taking pleasure as I watched him struggle to conquer roles that were choreographed for me, just as I had had to struggle to conquer the roles of the nineteenth century."

he failed to rebound from his heart surgery, but his eyesight was dimming and he was losing his sense of balance. Jerome Robbins visited him at home one day and found him with "hair astray, one eye black & very old and fragile looking—his Don Quixote come off the stage to visit him." Though the company put on a Tchaikovsky Festival and a second Stravinsky Festival, Balanchine's contributions, *Mozartiana* excepted, were undistinguished. And then, all at once, there were none: he entered Roosevelt Hospital at the end of 1982, weakened by a pair of rib-cracking falls in his apartment. Unable to work, he passed his days listening to music, receiving guests, and allowing Solomon Volkov to interview him for a book about Tchaikovsky. It was better than nothing, but not nearly enough. "You know," he told his doctor, "I still hear pretty music, and I see people doing things. But you can't tell them, you have to show them."

Though no one knew it, Balanchine was suffering from Creutzfeldt-Jakob disease, a deadly viral infection that gradually destroys the brain of its victims.* Years before, he had gone to Paul Niehans's clinic in Switzerland for rejuvenating injections of sheep-placenta extract, the same "cellular therapy" that Charlie Chaplin,

---

*Mad cow disease is caused by a variant of the Creutzfeldt-Jakob virus.

Winston Churchill, Noël Coward, Somerset Maugham, and Pope Pius XII had once received. Such treatments were the Viagra of their day, and it seems more than likely that Balanchine had sought them out as a way of enhancing his sexual potency. But they can also be a source of infection, and it may well be that Balanchine contracted the slow-developing, invariably fatal disorder as a result of the treatment he presumably sought in order to make himself more attractive to one or the other of the young women he pursued—an unimaginably grotesque irony.

Whatever the cause of his sickness, he knew he was dying, and his final reflections were by turns philosophical and despairing. "Love is a very important thing in a man's life, especially toward the end," he told Volkov. "More important than art." As for his art, he claimed to be pessimistic about the prospects for its survival. Ballets, he had always said, were like butterflies: "A breath, a memory, then gone." That did not stop him from repeatedly revising the steps of such now-classic dances as *Apollo, Serenade,* and *The Four Temperaments* to bring them into ever more exact accord with his wishes, or working with Merrill Brockway and Emile Ardolino on a series of PBS telecasts in which New York City Ballet danced meticulously rehearsed performances of *Prodigal Son, The Four Temperaments,* "Emeralds," *Stravinsky Violin Concerto, Chaconne,* and other ballets, ensuring that later generations of dancers and dancegoers would know what they had looked like under his supervision. But now he was skeptical about their survival. "When I die, everything should vanish," he said to Rudolf Nureyev. "A new person should come and impose his own things."

Who would it be? Jerome Robbins did not care to assume Balanchine's enormous administrative burden, though he did expect to be asked. Balanchine had hinted to various people that Peter Martins, who had choreographed his first dance in 1978 and was made one of the company's four ballet masters (together with Balanchine, Robbins, and John Taras) three years later, should succeed him, but he had never made his preference official. "Look," he warned Martins, "nobody is going to hand it to you. You're going to have to take it, you're going to have to fight for it." Some time in the fall of 1982, he asked Barbara Horgan to summon Orville Schell and Gillian Attfield, the chairman and president of the NYCB board, to his hospital room. According to Horgan, he told them, "I want Peter to be director. Don't give it to Lincoln. He'll destroy it." The following March, the *New York Times* reported that Robbins had "turned down an offer to be the company's artistic director," and he hit the ceiling. "What do you mean, you offered it to me?" Robbins asked Schell. "Who offered it to me? When did you offer it to me? When did I refuse?" In the end, the board voted to make Martins and Robbins co-ballet masters in chief; Martins would run the company from day to day, while Robbins was given complete control over his own ballets, with Balanchine as ballet master emeritus.

None of it mattered to Balanchine. His memory had been fading for weeks, and now he was losing the power of speech as well. "I would just sit on the bed," wrote Farrell, "holding his hand while he slept, but as soon as I rose to go, his hand would grip mine more tightly." Karin von Aroldingen saw him most often, but most of the many women he had loved made the pilgrimage to his bedside. Tamara Geva was the last. "One day I found him clutching a small icon in the palm of his hand," she said. "He brought it to my face and repeated several times, 'Must believe ... must believe ...' and closed his eyes. With every hour he seemed to grow farther away into the distance, like a shrinking shadow." All his life he had had the faith of a child. Now it was all he had left.

Balanchine's ballets, early and late, are full of unsettling images of loss. *Serenade* ends with a processional in which a woman left alone by the hand of fate is carried to her own destiny. In *Liebeslieder Walzer*, a woman appears to die in the arms of her partner; in *La Valse*, the partner is death. Even Apollo's triumphant ascent to Olympus was also a farewell to Earth. That, too, was part of his vision. Unlike Orpheus, whose terrible fate he had choreographed, Balanchine took for granted that earthly love must end in separation. Like the inescapable evanescence of choreography, loss was part of the cycle of life: "Choreography is like cooking or gardening. Not like painting, because painting stays. Dancing disintegrates. Like a garden. Lots of roses come up, and in the evening they're gone. Next day, the sun comes up. It's life. I'm connected to what is part of life." Only a fool, he knew, sought to prevent the inevitable.

In 1976 he added a coda to "Emeralds," a pas de sept in which the principal dancers of the ballet enact the stately sorrow of the incidental music Gabriel Fauré composed to accompany the death of Mélisande in Maurice Maeterlinck's *Pelléas et Mélisande.* At the very end, the ballerinas slip into the wings, vanishing like mist burned off by the morning sun, while their deserted cavaliers, left alone on the stage, sink down on one knee and gesture skyward in salute to . . . what? He never said.

TAMARA GEVA LEFT HIM on the afternoon of April 29. He died at four the next morning. After a lifetime of movement, he was still at last.

7 · HOME OF THE CLASSICS

· ·

*T*HAT AFTERNOON the entrance to the New York State Theater was flanked by sprays of lilacs, roses, and lilies. It was an ordinary Saturday matinee, one ballet by Balanchine and two by Robbins. Before the dancing started, a visibly shaken Lincoln Kirstein stepped before the curtain. "I don't have to tell you," he told the audience, "that Mr. B is with Mozart and Tchaikovsky and Stravinsky." Many of those who grieved took comfort in the fact that his ballets were being danced all over New York on what Arlene Croce would describe in the *New Yorker* as "the darkest week in the history of the company—in the history of ballet in America." The School of American Ballet was performing *Western Symphony* at its spring workshop; American Ballet Theatre had *Symphonie Concertante*, a Mozart ballet made in 1947 for Tanaquil Le Clercq and Diana Adams, on its Monday-night program. *On Your Toes* was playing on Broadway. And on the night of his death, the eve of Palm Sunday, Suzanne Farrell danced the adagio of *Symphony in C,* partnered by Peter Martins.

The next day Balanchine's body was brought to the Cathedral of Our Lady of the Sign, where mourners filed past the plain wooden coffin for more than an hour after the long service ended. Then a hearse carried it to a Long Island cemetery, where Farrell, Geva, Danilova, Tallchief, Le Clercq, Aroldingen, and Allegra Kent threw white roses into his open grave. The rest of New York read his obituaries in the morning papers, and in the days and weeks to come, virtually every important magazine in America would bid him a lengthy farewell.

The will he had drawn up after his heart attack was simple, for he had few assets. "What are you saving for?" he had told his dancers, urging them not to hold back. "It's like telling very young people, 'Put $5 a week in the bank and when you are eighty-seven, you'll have $5,000.' And everybody thinks, 'Oh, what I'll do then, not thinking that maybe then $5,000 will be worth 50 cents. Look at me: I'm there already—old, I mean—and I don't have a penny in the bank. I buy my wine and I drink it." It was the barest of exaggerations. He had no portfolio, no annuities, no insurance policies, nothing but two apartments, two gold watches, the balances in his checking and savings accounts, and the rights to his ballets, which he divided up among fourteen legatees, all of them wives, lovers, colleagues, and friends. *Serenade, Liebeslieder Walzer, Stravinsky Violin Concerto,* and *Vienna Waltzes* were left to Aroldingen; *Barocco* and *Orpheus* to Kirstein; *Don Quixote* to Farrell (he had already given her *Meditation*); *A Midsummer Night's Dream* to Adams; *Firebird* to Robbins; *Duo Concertant* to Kay Mazzo; *Symphony in C* to Betty Cage. The American rights to most of the remaining dances went to Le Clercq, while the foreign rights were shared by Aroldingen and Barbara Horgan, who also inherited all other dances not mentioned in the will. Nothing went to Martins or to New York City Ballet. It took three years for the will to be proved and the Internal Revenue Service satisfied with the final accounting, which placed the total taxable value of his estate at just under $1.2 million, $550,000 of which consisted of the estimated worth of the ballets.

In 1987 Horgan and Aroldingen set up a trust to administer the rights to Balanchine's ballets, and most of the other legatees chose to participate, as did New York City Ballet, which agreed to pay a flat annual fee in return for the right to continue dancing the ballets controlled by the trust. Under Horgan's direction, the

Balanchine Trust determines which companies will be allowed to perform the choreographer's work. While its financial terms are reasonable, even generous, the trust imposes rigorous rehearsal standards on companies licensed to perform the seventy-five-odd ballets it controls. These ballets must in turn be staged by authorized *répétiteurs,* and companies that fail to maintain them properly can (and do) have their licenses revoked. The Balanchine Trust is in large part responsible for the steadily increasing frequency with which Balanchine's ballets are performed worldwide. No less noteworthy, though, are the numerous ballet companies, most of them based in America, that are led by New York City Ballet alumni. These "Balanchine companies," as they are known, include San Francisco Ballet, Dance Theatre of Harlem, Pacific Northwest Ballet, Miami City Ballet, and Carolina Ballet. All dance Balanchine's ballets constantly and for the most part convincingly, and by the nineties many New York–based dancegoers had begun to wonder whether the city long known as "the dance capital of the world" was now no more than primus inter pares in the decentralized world of post-Balanchine ballet.

Two lists tell the tale. In 2004, the centennial of Balanchine's birth, American Ballet Theatre, the Australian Ballet, the Bolshoi, the Croatian National Ballet, the Finnish National Ballet, the Grand Théâtre de

Bordeaux, Het Nationale Ballet of Holland, the Kirov Ballet, the Norwegian National Ballet, Paris Opéra Ballet, the Royal Ballet, Stuttgart Ballet, Zurich Ballet, most of the Balanchine companies, and other companies in Cincinnati, Houston, Phoenix, and San Diego presented programs devoted solely to his work. During the same season, individual Balanchine ballets were danced by Alabama Ballet, Atlanta Ballet, Ballet Arlington, Ballet Pacifica, Ballet West, Boca Ballet Theatre, Boston Ballet, Colorado Ballet, Diablo Ballet, Grand Rapids Ballet, the Joffrey Ballet, Kansas City Ballet, Louisville Ballet, Pennsylvania Ballet, Pittsburgh Ballet Theatre, Sacramento Ballet, Texas Ballet, Washington Ballet, and companies in Canada, China, Denmark, England, Italy, Portugal, Puerto Rico, Scotland, South Africa, and Sweden.

As for Balanchine's company, critics and dance-goers have been wrangling for years over whether Peter Martins has been a good steward of his legacy. His position was impossible: no one could replace Mr. B, though Martins did his best, choreographing one or two new ballets each season, some clearly influenced by the example of the master, others just as clearly representing his struggle to break free from that smothering influence. After a few years, though, certain critics began to complain that many of Balanchine's own ballets had started to go out of focus. "For the first time since Balanchine's death, the company didn't appear to know how it got where it is, or where it was going," Arlene Croce wrote in 1988. (Martins asked Robert Gottlieb, then the editor of the *New Yorker*, to resign from the NYCB board after her piece was published.) At the same time, other prominent journalists continued to write approvingly of the company and its new ballet master in chief, though the voices of dissent grew more emphatic, never more so than when Suzanne Farrell, who had retired from dancing in 1989 to become a company coach, was fired four years later. She had previously given an interview in which she criticized NYCB for making so little use of her. "I never dreamed I would live to see the day when I didn't work for New York City Ballet," she told a reporter. Instead, she began staging Balanchine's ballets under the auspices of Washington's Kennedy Center, an experimental venture that over time evolved into Farrell's own Washington-based touring troupe, Suzanne Farrell Ballet.

Meanwhile, New York City Ballet soldiered on, launching the Diamond Project, a biennial festival of new choreography, and responding to declining ticket sales by cutting back its performing schedule. One by one, the last remaining dancers who had worked with Balanchine retired (or were let go), and with each departure his direct influence over the company's style was further diminished, though his ballets remained central to the NYCB repertory. Kirstein died in 1996, Robbins in 1998, and with their passing a long-dying age finally breathed its last. New York City Ballet had survived its founders. Now it was on its own.

DESPITE BALANCHINE'S continuing ubiquity in the world of ballet, his legacy is fragile. Dance notation is imperfect, *répétiteurs* fallible, video recordings ambiguous (though indispensable), while ballet itself has a problematic place among the arts. W. H. Auden, for all his admiration of Balanchine, dismissed it as a "very, very minor art," undeniably delightful but nonetheless trivial by comparison with poetry or opera. Though he spoke as a provocateur, Auden had a point. Only a handful of premodern ballets continue to be danced in their original form, and fewer still are indisputably major works of art. By and large, nineteenth-century ballet is remembered more for its music than its steps, just as we know more about the Ballets Russes' costumes than its choreography. It is worth remembering that there have only been two extended periods when ballet was at the forefront of Western cultural consciousness. Such was the case in the twenties, but that was solely because of the Ballets Russes, and Diaghilev's death sent ballet into a tailspin that lasted until the founding of Ballet Theatre in 1940 and the subsequent emergence of

George Balanchine as a dominant figure in twentieth-century dance. By the sixties few would have thought to question the value of ballet, but the death of Balanchine marked the beginning of a slow retreat that has yet to be reversed.

Though every art form goes through periods of stasis, to examine the track record of ballet in the twentieth century is to be struck by how few world-class creators it has produced. Diaghilev was an impresario, not a choreographer, and next to none of the works for which he served as midwife outlived him. Fokine's *Petrushka* and Nijinsky's *L'Après-midi d'un faune* survive more as ideas than actual ballets. Massine's once-celebrated dances are now revived only as occasional novelties, while Nijinska's *Les Biches* and *Les Noces,* though perfectly viable, have never quite succeeded in making their way into ballet's working repertory. Then came Balanchine—and after him, what? Or, to put it another way, were there any other twentieth-century ballet choreographers of like stature?

If a choreographer's stature can be measured by the frequency with which his work is performed by companies other than his own, the answer is no. New York City Ballet continues to perform most of Jerome Robbins's best-known dances side by side with its encyclopedic Balanchine repertory, but Robbins was stingy about making them available to other companies during his lifetime, and it remains to be seen whether more than three or four of the best ones will achieve wider circulation now that he is gone. Similarly, a mere handful of Frederick Ashton's neoromantic story ballets are danced by companies other than London's Royal Ballet, whose commitment to preserving and protecting its Ashton repertory has long been inconsistent. As for Antony Tudor, only *Jardin aux Lilas, Pillar of Fire,* and (possibly) *Dark Elegies* are securely entrenched in the international repertory, with two or three other ballets receiving less frequent performances. Outside of a sprinkling of lesser efforts by the likes of John Cranko, Agnes de Mille, and Kenneth MacMillan, surprisingly little else survives of the thousands of ballets made between the deaths of Diaghilev in 1929 and Balanchine in 1983. Then as now, the vast majority of the new works seen each season were choreographed by the artistic directors of the companies that premiered them, and were never seen anywhere else.*

This peculiar state of affairs is taken for granted by dancegoers, perhaps because many of them know

---

*Too many of those same artistic directors were (and are) persistently reluctant to invite younger choreographers to work with their companies, thus making it all the more difficult for promising new talents to emerge.

comparatively little about other art forms and thus are unaware of just how peculiar it is. But suppose that your entire knowledge of modern art derived from repeated visits to a museum whose permanent collection consisted of two dozen Matisses, ten paintings by Stuart Davis, six by Vuillard, three by Max Beckmann, and one each by, say, Wassily Kandinsky, Chaim Soutine, Walter Sickert, Grant Wood, and Pavel Tchelitchev, plus a rotating exhibit of new work by the museum's own director. What conclusions would you draw about the importance of modern art—or, for that matter, of Matisse?

To those who know little of dance, it may seem perverse to compare the greatest painter of the modern era with any choreographer, however gifted. But put aside for a moment the matter of Balanchine's standing in the larger world of art and consider this question: is it possible that he poured his prodigal energies into a pond too small to hold them? And if that is the case, do his dances, no matter how good they were, have a future? Few historians of dance have failed to note that from the sixties on, the creative energy in dance has been found primarily in modern dance. Merce Cunningham, Paul Taylor, Twyla Tharp, Mark Morris: these are the choreographers whose work has had the deepest impact on today's audiences. By contrast, none of the many ballet choreographers who danced for Balanchine has made more than a modest impression on the public at large. Peter Martins and Helgi Tomasson, who runs San Francisco Ballet, are the most prolific, but their ballets have mostly failed to be taken up by other companies. Nor has the situation changed greatly in recent years. At the present moment, the only full-time classical choreographer widely acknowledged as a major artist in the making is Christopher Wheeldon, who danced for New York City Ballet in the nineties but is too young to have known or worked with Balanchine.*

All this matters because the survival of Balanchine's ballets requires more than their mere archival preservation, whether on videotape or in dance notation. For them to live, they must be *danced*, not only by Balanchine companies steeped in the master's style but by ballet companies of every other kind and persuasion. Such companies cannot flourish if ballet comes to be seen as "a very, very minor art" dominated by revivals and repetitions of *Giselle, Swan Lake,* and *Sleeping Beauty,* any more than theater can live by Sophocles and Aristophanes alone. Should that happen, Balanchine's

---

*Robert Weiss, a New York City Ballet dancer who went on to lead Pennsylvania Ballet and found Carolina Ballet, is also making Balanchine-influenced dances of exceptionally high quality, but they are as yet rarely seen outside North Carolina, where his company is based.

attempts to modernize the language of ballet will prove to have been historically interesting but ultimately insignificant, the sunset of the classical tradition in dance.

On the other hand, it is also possible that we have reached the end of the beginning of the history of dance as a serious artistic medium, and that Balanchine will be remembered not as its last giant but its first, the founding father who took the rudimentary steps of classical ballet and transformed them into a modern language capable of expressing feelings of the utmost subtlety and complexity. Seen from that perspective, nineteenth-century ballet might someday come to resemble pre-Renaissance music or painting before Giotto—by no means unimportant, but mainly of interest to specialists—while Balanchine's primacy among modern ballet choreographers would become less isolating and more plausible, rather like that of Shakespeare among the playwrights of the Elizabethan era. If this is indeed the case, then the story of George Balanchine and his ballets has only just started to be told.

ON THE EVENING of the hundredth anniversary of Balanchine's birth, I went to the New York State Theater to watch New York City Ballet dance *Apollo, Prodigal Son,* and *Serenade.* It was bitterly cold in Manhattan, but the lobby was full of familiar faces: balletomanes and critics, aging ballerinas and budding young dancers, old friends of Balanchine and novice choreographers looking for inspiration. Though I'd seen all three ballets the week before, I couldn't imagine staying home. I had witnessed most of the great occasions since Balanchine's death—the company's fiftieth-anniversary celebration, Suzanne Farrell's last *Vienna Waltzes* and Jerome Robbins's last bow, the memorial services for Robbins and Tanaquil Le Clercq—and so I thought it right to be on hand to celebrate the birthday of the man who opened my eyes to ballet.

On paper it was just another repertory night, the kind that rarely inspires anything remotely approaching a sense of occasion, but no sooner were the lights lowered than I knew something was different. The orchestra launched into the fanfarelike introduction to *Apollo*, the curtain flew up to reveal Nikolaj Hübbe standing at center stage in front of a Balanchine-blue cyclorama, and I felt my skin prickle. As Hübbe strummed the fake lyre he held in his hands, I thought of how Balanchine liked to tell his dancers that he'd been talking to Stravinsky—or Tchaikovsky—the night before. Once such tales had made me smile, but at last I had an inkling of what he meant. The evening was full of uncanny encounters and events: the mysterious message that Calliope scribbles in her hand and shows to Apollo, the ominous flapping of the Dark Angel's wings at the end of *Serenade*, the terrible moment when a mob of bald-headed goons strips the Prodigal Son naked, their hands skittering over his limp body like the paws of greedy mice. All had sprung from the mind and body of the man we were there to honor. How could anyone doubt his presence, real or unreal?

It was one of those evenings when past and present are hooked together like the cars of a speeding train. The company Balanchine had founded was dancing his three oldest surviving ballets in the house he had built. *Apollo* was danced in the black-and-white version of 1979, but *Prodigal Son* looked much the way it did on the stage of the Théâtre Sarah-Bernhardt in 1929, right down to Rouault's thickly brushed backdrops. The dancers included Darci Kistler, Balanchine's last protégée, now married to Peter Martins, and Kyra Nichols, who in the hard years since Balanchine's death had become the outstanding exponent of the poised, transparent poetry of gesture of which he dreamed his whole life long. An old man sitting next to me reminisced out loud about seeing Edward Villella dance the Prodigal Son, and I in turn recalled my first *Serenade*, performed by Dance Theatre of Harlem at City Center, where I sat in the cheapest seats in the highest balcony, wondering if anything in the world was half so beautiful. Miniatures of Russian vodka were handed out in the second intermission, and after the last bow of the night was taken, Martins and Barbara Horgan came onstage to lead us in a birthday toast. "What he gave us," Martins said, "is all about love. There are young dancers on this stage who were not born when Mr. B died, and they love him." We raised our plastic glasses, the orchestra thundered out a fanfare, and balloons dropped from the fifth ring. As we filed out, the man who remembered Villella shook a finger in my face. "Your grandchildren will see these ballets," he said.

And will they? Balanchine himself affected to believe that his ballets would not long outlive him, at least not in any recognizable form. But he also founded New York City Ballet and the School of American Ballet, which exist to preserve authentic versions of his work and teach the techniques necessary to dance it idiomatically. And though he was not the first choreographer to start a company or a school, what sets him apart is the existence of the worldwide network of other institutions and individuals whose purpose is to disseminate authentic versions of his ballets as widely as possible and give them a permanent life in repertory. No other ballet choreographer has attracted so many followers, and no other choreographic oeuvre has been the subject of so thoroughgoing and committed an attempt at long-term preservation.

The Balanchine companies are not the only first-rate ballet companies in America, but their common emphasis on Balanchine, and the quality with which they stage his work, is a development of near-unprecedented significance, a sign that his style may be evolving into a lingua franca for ballet in the twenty-first century, just as the Franco-Russian style of classic ballet supplied a firm foundation on which the tradition-steeped Balanchine was able to build his neoclassical idiom. It helps, of course, that most of his dances are well suited to the restrictive circumstances under which repertory ballet is presented in this country. Because a dance like *Concerto Barocco* requires no set and no costumes beyond the simplest of practice clothes, it is relatively cheap to produce. Nor does the plotless *Barocco* need elaborate theatrical direction to make its effect: it contains no knowing looks, no labyrinthine subtexts, just music and steps. And unlike the myriad dialects of modern dance, the steps of classical ballet are a universal language, meaning that Balanchine's ballets, radically innovative though they are, can be executed by any technically proficient classical company.

"You know, these are my ballets," Balanchine told Rosemary Dunleavy, New York City Ballet's ballet mistress. "In the years to come they will be rehearsed by other people. They will be danced by other people. But no matter what, they are still my ballets." Of all the self-contradictory things he said about his work, that one seems to me closest to the truth. In the years since

I saw my first *Barocco*, I have taken countless friends to see their first Balanchine ballets, in New York and elsewhere, and watched them weep with joy at the sight of blurry, infirm performances far removed from the way such works look when lovingly set by first-string *répétiteurs* on meticulously rehearsed companies. That's as it should be: Balanchine's best ballets are sturdy enough to make their effect in any kind of performance. Whether the dancing is good or bad, accurate or approximate, they are still *his* ballets, and always will be.

I wish I could speak with absolute certainty about their future, but the jury of posterity is still out—and some highly knowledgeable observers have expressed skepticism about their prospects for survival. Frederick Ashton, for one, said that he "feared for the future" of Balanchine's plotless dances, which he believed to be inherently more difficult to maintain in repertory than story ballets, and which he thought might slowly disintegrate once Balanchine was no longer alive to rehearse them. That they *deserve* to live and flourish, however, seems to me beyond question. Like all the greatest art, George Balanchine's ballets take our innermost feelings and make them universal: laughter and dread, anguish and exaltation, love, death, and transcendence. They simultaneously arrest the eye and mind. After spending countless hours looking at dozens of them, I have come to believe that their creator was not merely the greatest ballet choreographer of the twentieth century, but the only one to have left behind a substantial body of work that deserves to be remembered in the same way we remember the work of Matisse or Stravinsky. And while I'm sure the balletomanes of 1929 felt the same way about the glittering repertory of the Ballets Russes, Balanchine's lean, stripped-down dances, unlike Diaghilev's evanescent spectacles, were built to last. This is not to say they can thrive in a vacuum, but the world of ballet is full of talented men and women determined to make sure that *Apollo, Serenade,* and *Prodigal Son* last at least as long as *The Red Studio* or *The Rite of Spring.* I wouldn't be at all surprised if my grandchildren see them—and their grandchildren, too.

Books about Balanchine

....

Balanchine, George. *Balanchine's Complete Stories of the Great Ballets.* Edited by Francis Mason. Revised and enlarged version. New York: Doubleday, 1977. Ghostwritten by Mason, but Balanchine's first-person "contributions" have the ring of authenticity.

Bentley, Toni. *Winter Season: A Dancer's Journal* (with a new preface by the author). Gainesville: University Press of Florida, 2003. A sensitive diary-memoir by a former member of the NYCB corps, originally published in 1982.

Buckle, Richard. *Buckle at the Ballet: Selected Criticism.* New York: Atheneum, 1980. Lively performance reviews by the first English dance critic to recognize Balanchine's significance.

———. *Diaghilev.* New York: Atheneum, 1979. The standard biography.

Buckle, Richard, in collaboration with John Taras. *George Balanchine, Ballet Master.* New York: Random House, 1988. The only full-length biography of Balanchine published to date. Well-meaning and often useful, but insufficiently detailed or thoughtful.

Choreography by George Balanchine: A Catalogue of Works. New York: Eakins Press/Viking, 1984. The definitive catalogue raisonée.

Croce, Arlene. *Writing in the Dark, Dancing in* The New Yorker. New York: Farrar, Straus & Giroux, 2000. A selection of Croce's dance reviews, second only in importance to Edwin Denby's *Dance Writings* as a chronicle of Balanchine's ballets in performance.

Danilova, Alexandra. *Choura: The Memoirs of Alexandra Danilova.* New York: Knopf, 1986. The autobiography of Balanchine's "second wife."

Denby, Edwin. *Dance Writings.* Edited by Robert Cornfield and William Mackay. New York: Knopf, 1986. The collected writings of the greatest dance critic of the twentieth century, including reviews of Balanchine premieres and performances of the forties and fifties.

Farrell, Suzanne, with Toni Bentley. *Holding on to the Air: An Autobiography.* New York: Summit, 1990. A candid memoir by Balanchine's last muse (though unexpectedly unilluminating about the ballets she danced).

Garafola, Lynn, with Eric Foner, eds. *Dance for a City: Fifty Years of the New York City Ballet.* New York: Columbia, 1999. The catalog of the New-York Historical Society's 1999 exhibition.

Garis, Robert. *Following Balanchine.* New Haven: Yale University Press, 1995. A quirky autobiographical chronicle of a critic's evolving interest in Balanchine's work.

Geva, Tamara. *Split Seconds: A Remembrance.* New York: Harper & Row, 1972. The autobiography of Balanchine's first wife.

Haggin, B. H. *Discovering Balanchine.* New York: Horizon, 1981. A brief reminiscence of the choreographer by one of his earliest and most passionate critical advocates.

Joseph, Charles M. *Stravinsky and Balanchine: A Journey of Invention.* New Haven: Yale University Press, 2002. The first study of Balanchine's ballets written by a trained musician with extensive knowledge of dance (as well as the first book about Balanchine to make use of his and Stravinsky's papers). Essential reading, though occasionally difficult for nonmusicians.

Jowitt, Deborah. *Jerome Robbins: His Life, His Theater, His Dance.* New York: Simon & Schuster, 2004. A primary-source biography of Robbins, the first to be based on his papers. Emphasizes his work (though not to the exclusion of his life) and contains previously unpublished information about Balanchine and NYCB drawn from his correspondence and journals.

Kent, Allegra. *Once a Dancer... : An Autobiography.* New York: St. Martin's, 1997. Discursive but highly readable.

Kirstein, Lincoln. *The New York City Ballet.* New York: Knopf, 1973. The profusely illustrated "official" history of the company, written from Kirstein's idiosyncratic perspective. (Beware of the "quotations from an imaginary diary, such as might have been kept but in fact was not.")

————. *By With To & From: A Lincoln Kirstein Reader.* Edited by Nicholas Jenkins. New York: Farrar, Straus & Giroux, 1991. Includes articles and diary entries about Balanchine and ballet, plus a biographical essay by the editor. (The account of Kirstein's first meeting with Balanchine, published in *Mosaic,* his 1994 memoir, is based on the authentic diary entries included here.)

Lawrence, Greg. *Dance with Demons: The Life of Jerome Robbins.* New York: G. P. Putnam's Sons, 2001. The first Robbins biography, based in part on interviews but written without access to Robbins's papers. Gossipy, interesting, unreliable.

Martins, Peter, and Robert Cornfield. *Far from Denmark.* Boston: Little, Brown, 1982. An account of Martins's years as an NYCB dancer.

Mason, Francis. *I Remember Balanchine: Recollections of the Ballet Master by Those Who Knew Him.* New York: Doubleday, 1991. Eighty-five oral-history interviews with dancers, colleagues, and friends. Indispensable.

Mazo, Joseph H. *Dance Is a Contact Sport.* New York: E. P. Dutton, 1974. New York City Ballet in 1973, seen from the inside by a journalist who spent the season watching the company rehearse and perform. Naively enthusiastic but nonetheless useful as an introduction to the workings of a ballet company.

McDonagh, Don. *George Balanchine.* Boston: Twayne, 1983. A critical monograph containing scene-by-scene descriptions of several Balanchine ballets.

Milstein, Nathan, and Solomon Volkov. *From Russia to the West: The Musical Memoirs and Reminiscences of Nathan Milstein.* Translated by Antonina W. Bouis. New York: Limelight, 1991. The autobiography of the famous violinist-raconteur, including a long and affectionate chapter about his close friendship with Balanchine.

Reynolds, Nancy. *Repertory in Review: 40 Years of the New York City Ballet.* New York: Dial, 1977. An extensively annotated catalog of the NYCB repertory, including interview material and excerpts from contemporary performance reviews.

Schorer, Suki, with Russell Lee. *Suki Schorer on Balanchine Technique.* New York: Knopf, 1999. An illustrated manual by an NYCB ballerina who became one of the School of American Ballet's most admired teachers. Technical but (largely) accessible to the layman.

Tallchief, Maria, with Larry Kaplan. *Maria Tallchief: America's Prima Ballerina.* New York: Henry Holt, 1997. The autobiography of Balanchine's "official" third wife.

Taper, Bernard. *Balanchine: A Biography.* Berkeley: University of California Press, 1984. An expanded and revised version of Taper's *New Yorker* profiles of Balanchine, mainly based on interviews with the choreographer. Frequently evasive about personal matters but invaluable as the source of many well-known Balanchine quotes and anecdotes (some of which were embroidered by Balanchine himself).

Taylor, Paul. *Private Domain: An Autobiography* (reissued with a new foreword by Terry Teachout). Pittsburgh: University of Pittsburgh, 1999. The autobiography of the

Balanchine of modern dance. Contains a vivid description of the creation and early performances of
Episodes, in which Taylor performed.

Tracy, Robert, with Sharon DeLano. *Balanchine's Ballerinas:
Conversations with the Muses.* New York: Linden Press/
Simon & Schuster, 1983. Transcripts of interviews
with nineteen women who danced for Balanchine,
all conducted during the choreographer's lifetime.
Sometimes interesting, but most of the subjects are un-
forthcoming about their personal relationships with
Balanchine.

Villella, Edward, with Larry Kaplan. *Prodigal Son: Dancing
for Balanchine in a World of Pain and Magic.* New York:
Simon & Schuster, 1992. The frankest of the various
memoirs by NYCB alumni, notable for its vivid accounts of how Balanchine made *A Midsummer Night's
Dream, Bugaku,* and "Rubies" and rehearsed *Apollo* and
Prodigal Son.

Volkov, Solomon. *Balanchine's Tchaikovsky: Interviews with
George Balanchine.* Translated by Antonina W. Bouis. New
York: Simon & Schuster, 1995. Balanchine's thoughts
about Tchaikovsky (and himself), skillfully edited by
Volkov into a first-person monologue. The only published interviews with Balanchine to have been originally conducted in Russian.

MANY OF BALANCHINE'S BALLETS were telecast during his
lifetime in performances supervised by the choreographer
and featuring members of the original casts. *Choreography by*

Balanchine (Nonesuch 79838-2 and 79839-2) is a pair of DVDs containing complete performances by New York City Ballet of *Chaconne,* "Emeralds," *The Four Temperaments, Prodigal Son,* and *Stravinsky Violin Concerto,* plus several shorter Balanchine ballets and excerpts from longer dances. The performances, originally telecast on PBS's *Dance in America* series, were videotaped in 1977.

Balanchine (Kultur D2448), a 156-minute documentary first seen in 1984, contains extended excerpts from *Agon, Apollo, Chaconne, The Four Temperaments, Ivesiana, Jewels, Liebeslieder Walzer, A Midsummer Night's Dream, Orpheus, Prodigal Son, Robert Schumann's "Davidsbündlertänze," Serenade, Square Dance, Stars and Stripes, Stravinsky Violin Concerto, Symphony in C,* and *Western Symphony,* plus interviews with Balanchine and shorter excerpts from other ballets. Featured dancers include Diana Adams, Jacques d'Amboise, Merrill Ashley, Mikhail Baryshnikov, Suzanne Farrell, Allegra Kent, Tanaquil Le Clercq, Peter Martins, Kay Mazzo, Suki Schorer, Maria Tallchief, Violette Verdy, and Patricia Wilde. (Balanchine is seen as Drosselmeyer in a brief scene from the 1958 telecast of *The Nutcracker.*)